A Cabinet of Curiosities
Five Episodes in
the Evolution of
American Museums

The Dodo used to walk around, / And take the sun and air. / The sun yet warms his native ground – / The Dodo is not there! / The voice which used to squawk and squeak / Is now for ever dumb – / Yet you may see his bones and beak / All in the Mu-se-um. / —Hilaire Belloc, *The Bad Child's Book of Beasts*

Five Episodes in

the Evolution of

American Museums

A Cabinet of Curiosities

described by

Whitfield J. Bell, Jr.

Clifford K. Shipton

John C. Ewers

Louis Leonard Tucker

Wilcomb E. Washburn

with an Introduction by

Walter Muir Whitehill

The University Press of Virginia

Charlottesville

Introduction

THIS book evolved from a session devoted to the history of museums at the Washington meeting of the American Historical Association on December 28, 1964, at which Clifford K. Shipton, Louis Leonard Tucker, and Wilcomb E. Washburn read papers.

Mr. Shipton described how the American Antiquarian Society, of which he is director—founded in 1812 with the broadest interest in "American Antiquities, natural, artificial and literary"—pioneered in archaeology and anthropology, but eventually completely abandoned its museum in order to concentrate its resources on the perfection of its library holdings. Mr. Tucker, at the time director of the Cincinnati Historical Society but now Assistant Commissioner for State History in the New York State Education Department, retrieved the long-forgotten history of the Western Museum of Cincinnati, which, established in 1820 with the loftiest scientific purposes, before long degenerated into a commercial peep show. Mr. Washburn presented extracts from a longer study concerning Joseph Henry's conception of the purpose of the Smithsonian Institution, which emphasized the increase of knowledge rather than its diffusion. As chairman, I tossed in a few homilies derived from *The East India Marine Society and the Peabody Museum of Salem: A Sesquicentennial History*, which I had written in 1949 for the one hundred and fiftieth anniversary of the oldest museum in continuous operation in the United States. The hundred and sixty-five years of the Peabody Museum vividly illustrate the stages in the transition from a shipmasters' cabinet of "natural and artificial curiosities" to a modern museum specializing in maritime history, the ethnology of the Pacific Islands and Japan, and the natural history of Essex County.

It was a lively and amusing afternoon, for the three panelists were literate as well as learned and were blessed with a sense of humor. No one in the audience went to sleep, and very few withdrew in search of other sessions. The American Museum of Natural History immediately expressed interest in the papers for its quarterly, *Curator,* and the University Press of Virginia for publication as a book. The papers as delivered were printed in *Curator,* VIII, no. 1 (1965), 5–54.

In this book two other friends have joined the panelists of the 1964 meeting: Whitfield J. Bell, Jr., who describes the cabinet of the American Philosophical Society, of which he is librarian, and John C. Ewers, sometime director of the Museum of History and Technology, United States National Museum, who has revived the memory of William Clark's Indian Museum in St. Louis, 1818–38. Mr. Tucker has amplified his paper, and Mr. Washburn has very substantially enlarged his account of Joseph Henry beyond the form printed in *Curator.* We now offer a five-course dinner, rather than a three, with substantially larger helpings, although the gastronomic intention and the style of cookery and service remain unchanged. First we present the experience of two of the oldest learned societies whose "cabinets," once considered valuable adjuncts to scholarly organizations, were in the end eliminated. Then we offer accounts of two early private proprietary museums, which attracted great popular interest in their time. William Clark's Indian Museum in St. Louis, opened in 1818, lasted for twenty years but was dispersed on his death. The Western Museum of Cincinnati, founded in 1820 with the most respectable scientific motives, stumbled, through catering to popular interest, into the category of a side show. Its decline reminds us of the perils of even a few oblations to bunkum and provides convincing proof that waxworks constitute the beginning of the descent to hell. Finally the account of Joseph Henry not only describes an important stage in the evolution of the Smithsonian Institution but gives food for thought on the relation of research to the housekeeping of objects and to popular education.

WALTER MUIR WHITEHILL

Boston, Massachusetts
October 1966

Contents

Illustrations

A Cabinet of Curiosities

Five Episodes in
the Evolution of
American Museums

exander, gardener at Thomas Penn's estate of Springettsbury, produced specimens of asbestos from Chester County and some leaves of the cassina from South Carolina, which was thought to be the same as Labrador tea. "These were ordered to be placed with the other Curiosities in the Hands of Owen Biddle untill a proper Place is provided to deposit them in." A few months later such a place was provided, or at least projected, when a committee were directed "to get made a Cabinet suitable for keeping the Curiosities &c. belonging to the Society."[4]

Meanwhile the American Philosophical Society, which had been founded by Franklin in 1743 but had died two or three years afterward, was resurrected by Dr. Thomas Bond, one of the original members.[5] It met regularly in 1767 and 1768, elected a large number of members, received written communications on subjects in science and the applications of science, and doubtless accumulated some natural and artificial curiosities. Robert Strettel Jones and Dr. Francis Alison each presented samples of wine from American grapes;[6] but as the specimens could be tested only by consuming them, they found no permanent place in the Society's cabinet.

It was soon apparent to reasonable men that Philadelphia was too small for two scientific academies; and in the early winter of 1768–69, after protracted diplomatic negotiations, the two societies united. The new organization's bylaws provided for the annual election

---

[4] *Ibid.*, March 25, Aug. 26, 1768. The word "cabinet" had two meanings in the eighteenth century: (1) a collection of specimens of natural history, of paintings, prints, and sculpture, and of instruments, machines, and mechanical models, especially if curious or unusual; and (2) the receptacle in which these articles, especially specimens of natural history, were preserved and exhibited. In this paper the first meaning of "cabinet" is used interchangeably with "museum."

[5] Brooke Hindle, *The Pursuit of Science in Revolutionary America, 1735–1789* (Chapel Hill, N.C., 1956), 127–45.

[6] Henry Phillips, Jr., ed., "Early Proceedings of the American Philosophical Society . . . to 1838," APS *Proceedings*, XXII, pt. 3 (1885), 15–16.

of officers, including three curators. The latters' duties were

> to take charge of, and preserve, all *Specimens of natural Productions*, whether of the ANIMAL, VEGETABLE or FOSSIL Kingdom; all Models of Machines and Instruments, and all other matters and things belonging to the Society, which shall be committed to them; to class and arrange them in their proper order, and to keep an exact list of them, with the names of the respective donors, in a book provided for that purpose; which book shall be laid before the Society, as often as called for.[7]

The first curators of the united Society under these regulations were Dr. Adam Kuhn, professor of botany at the College of Philadelphia, Dr. John Morgan, professor of the theory and practice of medicine at the College, and Lewis Nicola. Their successors in 1770 were Isaac Bartram, apothecary, Dr. Benjamin Rush, professor of chemistry in the College of Philadelphia, and Owen Biddle, watchmaker and astronomer.[8]

As the Society grew, its museum inevitably expanded. Perhaps the most numerous contributions in the years before the Revolution were natural curiosities. Specimens of asbestos came from Henry Hollingsworth of Maryland and from Andrew Oliver of Salem, Massachusetts. Dr. John Lorimer presented seeds and dried flowers from Florida, and George Gauld of Pensacola forwarded a shark's jaw and specimens of shagreen and porcupine fish. Dr. John Archer of Baltimore County, Maryland, sent the Society the stuffed skin of some kind of amphibious animal, which its captors described as "very active & springy as it did when persued leap five or six Yards on level Ground . . . [and] made the most use of its Tail in Leaping." What the creature was neither Archer nor the Philadelphia philosophers knew, and we can only guess that it may have been that species of salamander known as a hell-

---

[7] "Laws and Regulations," APS *Transactions*, I (1771), x.

[8] "List of Officers, 1769 to 1934," APS *Proceedings*, LXXIII (1934), 380–83.

bender. An important addition to the natural history cabinet was made in 1770 when the widow of William Johnson, who had been a teacher and traveling lecturer on science and a member of the Society, presented her husband's collection.[9]

Another kind of contribution to the cabinet of the Society during the first years of its existence was examples of native productions. Benjamin Peters gave a leather bowl of his own making. Wilhelm Stiegel, the glassmaker of Mannheim, Pennsylvania, presented samples of decanters, wine and beer glasses, and other articles from his factory. John Arbo of Bethlehem sent specimens of oils extracted from various vegetables and fruits. Closely related to such articles of domestic manufacture were models of improved tools, instruments, and machines, which usually accompanied verbal descriptions by the inventors. Thomas Gilpin of Pennsylvania and Maryland, for example, designed a horizontal windmill, and John Jones of Sussex County, Delaware, invented a mowing machine; both were described in communications to the Society, and each communication was accompanied by the model.[10]

Of possibly greater public interest than any of these, because they were of remote origin and thus mildly exotic, were the Indian snowshoes and hatchet that James Dickinson presented in 1772. This gift foreshadowed the interest the Society would soon take in the American Indians and the considerable number of exhibits there would soon be in its museum of the tools, weapons, and clothing of the western tribes.

During the first twenty years of its life the Society met in rented rooms with no proper facilities for preserving or exhibiting the collection. Furthermore, members sometimes borrowed books and articles for study and examination at home. The result could have

[9] Phillips, "Early Proceedings," *passim;* Archer to Robert Harris, Dec. 2, 1773, MS. Communications, I, 6.

[10] Robert P. Multhauf, *A Catalogue of Instruments and Models in the Possession of the American Philosophical Society* (Philadelphia, 1961), 42–43; Phillips, "Early Proceedings," 39.

been expected. In 1774 the Society had to direct the curators "to collect the Books and other Valuables belonging to the Society & place them in the Cabinet."[11]

The American Revolution interrupted the meetings of the Society for several years. The cabinet and library were both necessarily neglected during this period, and a good many articles were taken away by members and others, often for safekeeping, but without any record being made of the removals. Accordingly, one of the curators' first actions after the war was to survey the cabinet and take "immediate measures for preserving the same from further decay." What was finally done was to put the library, books of natural history, curiosities, and the like under David Rittenhouse's care; and Rittenhouse took them to his house until a more convenient place could be found for them.[12] Meanwhile, articles continued to come in—a piece of petrified wood, prints illustrating the history of the Revolution, calculi taken from the bellies of horses in Bedfordshire, specimens of writing on coconut leaves, a telescope, a scale, and a microscope.

Throughout these early years the objects in the Society's museum merely accumulated; they were not collected. Whatever anyone thought likely to interest the members was sent to the Society; no effort was made to acquire materials systematically to illustrate or provide data for study of subjects of special interest to the Society or its members. Interest was expressed in purchasing portions of Pierre E. du Simitière's collection; but it does not appear that anything came of this.[13] As for classification and organization, there were as yet hardly enough articles of a kind to make classification necessary or possible. And, since the Society still lacked permanent quarters of its own, articles in the collection were always liable to being mislaid or borrowed.

[11] APS Minutes, Feb. 18, 1774.
[12] *Ibid.*, March 6, April 4, Nov. 21, Dec. 5, 1783.
[13] *Ibid.*, Oct. 15, Nov. 12, 1784.

The construction of Philosophical Hall in 1785–89 changed this haphazard situation. The Society now had rooms of its own for meetings and for the permanent installation and exhibition of its library and cabinet. The business of the Society increased, and with the stepped-up activity the flow of books and curiosities rose from both domestic and foreign correspondents. William Henry of Lancaster, Pennsylvania, in 1785 presented a model of a wheel carriage, two pieces of crystal, and the large tusk and grinders of an unknown animal. "XY," identified only as a "friend," sent a model of an improved boiler. Matthias Barton sent shells and nuts from the Susquehanna, Indian darts, some bark of the water birch, and "a specimen of a bear's gut." An Army officer at Fort Vincennes sent a collection of fossils; a minister at Ringwood, New Jersey, sent petrified shells; a vial of petroleum from Oil Creek in western Pennsylvania came from one William Turnbull. St. John de Crèvecoeur, author of *Letters from an American Farmer*, presented a book made of roots and bark, and Samuel Vaughan, Jr., presented specimens of cinnamon and breadfruit and a goose quill. When the Society at last moved into its building in 1789, the curators were directed to arrange and catalogue all these articles, as well as the library, and place them in the Hall.[14]

The Hall was completed just as the federal government moved its offices from New York to Philadelphia. Because the building was only a few steps from the governmental offices and many officers of government were members of the Society, the Society's library and

[14] *Ibid.*, Feb. 5, 1790. A German lithographic stone, presented to the cabinet by the printer Thomas Dobson, was loaned to Dr. Samuel Brown and Bass Otis in 1819 for an experiment in lithography. Following suggestions of Brown and Dr. Thomas Cooper, Otis designed and executed a print of a small farmhouse "from beginning to end—from the drawing to the impression inclusive." It is generally considered the first American lithograph. It is reproduced, with a description of the process, in *Analectic Magazine*, XIV (1819), 67–73.

collections were sometimes called on by federal departments. The Secretary of War, for example, borrowed a map in 1793 "for the public use, and for the replacing of which I hereby pledge the US." A few years later the government borrowed an achromatic telescope for Andrew Ellicott, who was about to make a boundary survey. Even after the capital was moved to the District of Columbia, the Society continued to serve as a kind of national museum, library, and scientific academy. Ferdinand R. Hassler of the Coast and Geodetic Survey borrowed the Society's French standard weights and measures in 1817; and in 1828 Albert Gallatin borrowed some maps to be laid before the arbiter of the northeast boundary of the United States. They were returned twenty-four years later.[15]

Though the Society now had a building and thus a permanent abode, it had no staff. It operated entirely through elected officers and appointed committees. Most of these men were busy physicians, lawyers, merchants, farmers, and schoolmasters. The Philadelphia members could attend the bimonthly meetings more or less regularly, and, though always ready to show the building and its collections to a stranger with proper introductions, they could not attend at fixed hours. The usefulness of the growing library and cabinet were thus necessarily limited to members and a few others. A better arrangement was made in 1794 when Charles Willson Peale rented a major part of the Hall for personal occupancy and for his natural history museum. The lease contained a requirement that Peale should act as librarian and "as *depository* of the Models, drawings, plans, natural and artificial curiosities, and all their other property; and the same preserve in order, and exhibit at proper times, under the direction

[15] Henry Knox, Receipt to John Vaughan, April 26, 1793; Timothy Pickering and Andrew Ellicott, Receipt, Aug. 1796; Ferdinand R. Hassler, Receipt, Feb. 8, 1817; Albert Gallatin, Receipt, Dec. 26, 1828, Curators' Material (Not Catalogued [1964]). The return of the maps Gallatin borrowed is recorded in APS Minutes, May 21, Dec. 17, 1852.

of the Curators."[16] This agreement had obvious advantages to both Peale and the Society. The former got a good location at the center of town, the prestige of the Society's patronage, and the opportunity to relate his own and the Society's collections in ways that would enhance the educational and dramatic value of both. The Society received the services of a knowledgeable and tireless caretaker, a sort of resident agent, who would make the cabinet more generally accessible and introduce an element of plan and continuity into the library and museum which had been lacking before.

With the opening of the Ohio and Mississippi valleys the Society received a steadily increasing number of articles both of natural history and of Indian manufacture. George Turner, one of the judges of the Northwest Territory, made several gifts of Indian artifacts and antiquities. One lot in 1797 contained:

A pair of Indian boy's leggings from the Missouri.

A Calumet of Peace, ornamented with Porcupine's quills for Indians on the Missouri.

An Indian Conjuror's Mask, formed of the scalp, &c. of a Buffalo, from the Missouri.

An Arrow neatly headed with bone, from the Saukis Indians on the upper parts of the Mississippi.

Eight of the Arrows commonly used by the Miami and neighbouring Indians.

A Stone Pestle used by the Indians formerly, for pounding corn and jerking flesh.

A Stone Hatchet formerly in use among the Savages.

A Specimen of petrified supposed Buffalo dung, from the Rapids of the Ohio.

Fine fossil coal, from Cincinnati, on the Ohio.

Part of one among thirty or forty trees, all completely petrified, from 212 miles up the Tenessee river.

An Indian bowl, taken out of the bed of the Tenessee.

An Oviform stone, from the Wabash.

[16] APS Minutes, May 30, 1794; Charles C. Sellers, *Charles Willson Peale*, Vol. II: *Later Life (1790–1827)* (Philadelphia, 1947), 60, 84.

Marine Shells and perforated bones, taken out of an ancient Indian grave on the Great Kanahwa.

American Porcupine Quills dyed with different colours.

Quills of the same animal with their natural colour.

Skin of an Indian taken from the side.

Part of the Sea-Otter skin, from its flank, where the fur is shortest, being part of a blanket coat brought from the Pacific coast by Dr. M'Kenzie, in 1794.

An American Swan's foot stuffed.

A Spear used by the Savages in killing Col. Chew, on the Ohio.

Various Indian Arrows from the North Western territory.

Specimen of Indian Sculpture in wood, resembling the Beaver; from the Kaskaskian nation.

A pair of Indian garters tipped with tin and Porcupine quills, from the Wabash.

Another pair from the Creek nation.

An Indian belt, from the Mississippi.[17]

Other Indian relics came from Colonel Winthrop Sargent, secretary of the Northwest Territory; John Heckewelder's daughter (moccasins and a tobacco pouch) ; the naturalist Thomas Nuttall; Redmond Conyngham, a local historian of Harrisburg, Pennsylvania; and others. Dr. Daniel Drake in 1818 presented a number of articles taken from an Indian burial mound in Ohio.

The West was also the source of some of the more dramatic exhibits in natural history in the Society's cabinet. Hardly a year passed in the first quarter of the nineteenth century without a gift of fossils or the bones of prehistoric beasts. Thomas Jefferson, General James Wilkinson, and Judge H. Bry of Louisiana presented such specimens. Dr. Samuel Brown of Lexington, Kentucky, was a particularly frequent contributor to this section of the Society's museum. In 1802 he sent "a Portion of the Cranium and part of the horn of an animal supposed to be of the Bison kind," and followed

[17] APS *Transactions*, IV (1799), xxviii–xxx; APS Minutes, Feb. 10, 24, 1797.

this gift by others, not only of bones—in 1805 he for-warded the cranium and bones of a peccary—but also of minerals and even a Roman Catholic amulet found in the earth near Nashville.

Some of these prehistoric remains were in fact bones of the mammoth, as the mastodon was then called; still others were thought to be, for the mammoth was one of the most exciting topics in American natural history at the end of the eighteenth century. Whether the beast was extinct or might be yet found roaming in some remote part of the West was a question that had ex-cited scientists and theologians alike for fifty years. Since the middle of the eighteenth century French and English explorers in the Ohio Valley had been uncover-ing parts of a beast of enormous size and apparently terrifying habits. The traders George Croghan and George Morgan of Philadelphia collected bones of the animal at Big Bone Lick in Kentucky, sent some pieces to Franklin in London, where they were described by Dr. William Hunter in a paper in the *Philosophical Transactions* of the Royal Society, and gave other parts to Morgan's brother John, professor of medicine at the College of Philadelphia. When Dr. Christian F. Michaelis, surgeon with the Hessian troops in Amer-ica, asked in 1783 for pictures of the bones, Morgan took them to Charles Willson Peale to draw.[18] This assignment aroused Peale's interest in the subject, and for the next twenty years he and his son Rembrandt devoted a good deal of time and energy to finding a complete mastodon's skeleton. They succeeded at last in 1801; and the skeleton they unearthed became one of the most popular attractions in Peale's Museum in Philosophical Hall.[19]

Inevitably thoughtful persons wondered how like the elephant the mammoth might be. The Society could help here; in 1802 it elected the naturalist William

[18] Whitfield J. Bell, Jr., "A Box of Old Bones: A Note on the Identification of the Mastodon, 1766–1806," APS *Proceedings*, XCIII (1949), 169–77.
[19] Sellers, *C. W. Peale*, 127–44.

Roxburgh of Calcutta to membership and accompanied the announcement of his election with a request for a complete skeleton of a large Indian elephant. Roxburgh obtained one, and it was shipped to Philadelphia in 1805, with all charges defrayed by the Asiatic Society of Bengal. The Society directed that the skeleton be placed in the same room with Peale's mammoth so that its lesson might be conveyed to visitors with the greatest force.[20]

When Peale moved the last sections of his museum in 1811 from Philosophical Hall to the State House next door, the mammoth went with him. Alone, it was a sufficiently awe-inspiring exhibit, and Peale, with his instinct for the dramatic, made the most of it. The Indian elephant, left behind in Philosophical Hall, languished without its mate and was dismantled and packed away. In 1826 Peale asked for the loan of it; and, after some hesitation because Peale's Museum was now a commercial venture, the Society sent it to him.[21]

The interest of the Society's own paleontological collection was not measurably diminished by the removal of its elephant and Peale's mammoth to the State House. Many bones and fragments of bones of the mastodon remained; these were added to by both gifts and occasional purchases, and the originals were supplemented by casts and models. After the death in 1818 of Dr. Caspar Wistar, president of the Society, his

[20] William Roxburgh to John R. Coxe, Feb. 14, 1803, Dec. 12, 1804; Caspar Wistar to John Vaughan, April 26, 1803; Roxburgh to Vaughan, Dec. 29, 1803, Archives; APS Minutes, Jan. 17, 1806.

[21] APS Minutes, Sept. 15, Oct. 6, 1826. Rembrandt and Franklin Peale gave their receipt, on behalf of the Philadelphia Museum, for the bones of the knocked-down elephant (Curators' Material [Not Catalogued (1964)]). Upon the dissolution of Peale's Museum the elephant came back to the Society, which then placed it in the University of Pennsylvania; when the University surrendered the skeleton, the remains were deposited in the Academy of Natural Sciences (APS Minutes, May 19, 1843, June 19, 1845).

widow returned to the cabinet the articles he had borrowed. The list gives a hint of the size and character of
this portion of the collection:

55 bones belonging to the feet of the mammoth
 3 fragments of ribb of do.
50 bones belonging to the feet, legs & spine of the
   Unknown animal
12 fragments supposed to belong to the head of the
   mammoth
24 specimens of teeth of mammoth
13 fragments of teeth & defenses of different Animals
 3 fragments of the upper jaw of the mammoth containing teeth
 5 fragments of the lower jaw of do.
 6 fragments of the bony part of horns
 2 large horns
 2 large defenses
 2 fragments of smaller do.
 4 fragments of the heads of unknown Animals
 1 head Unknown[22]

Like some of the materials on ethnology and paleontology, parts of the collections in botany and mineralogy came from the West. In prestige of provenance the
collections of plants and minerals made by Lewis and
Clark on their transcontinental exploration stood first.
They had sent the materials to Jefferson, who was
president of the Society as well as of the United States;
and Jefferson forwarded them to Philadelphia with the
request that the seeds be given to William Hamilton of
"Woodlands," so that he might plant them in his gar-
dens and report on what they produced.[23] Another important botanical collection was the herbarium of the
Pennsylvania botanist Gotthilf Muhlenberg of Lancaster; nine members subscribed $500 to purchase it for
the Society.[24] In 1834 Dr. Charles W. Short of Louisville donated an herbarium containing 535 specimens,

[22] John Vaughan, Receipt for fossil remains, April 15, 1818,
Curators' Material, 1801–97.
[23] APS Minutes, Nov. 15, 1805.   [24] *Ibid.,* Feb. 20, 1818.

gathered chiefly in the southern and western states; and seven years later he presented a second herbarium which contained specimens not in the first.[25]

In the years following 1800 the Society received several collections of minerals. Thomas P. Smith, a promising young chemist who died untimely, bequeathed his collection, which consisted principally of specimens collected in Europe.[26] Dr. James Woodhouse, professor of chemistry in the University of Pennsylvania, also bequeathed his mineralogical collection to the Society.[27] Mrs. Benjamin Smith Barton allowed the Society to take specific items from her late husband's cabinet.[28] To increase and complete its mineral collections the Society as early as 1805 authorized the curators to exchange duplicates; and in 1807 Dr. James Mease offered any of his duplicates lacking in the Society's holdings.[29] In the same year Juan Manuel Ferrer of Vera Cruz made a gift of a box of minerals; and there were many gifts of single specimens of interest, such as Moreau de Saint-Méry's piece of copper ore from Santo Domingo, and Dr. Samuel Brown's specimen of salt petre.

History and prehistory under a variety of aspects were generously represented in the cabinet of the Philosophical Society. Indeed the collection of Mexican and Central American antiquities was perhaps the most impressive in the Society's museum and was widely recognized as the finest on the North American continent. The larger part of this collection was presented to the Society in 1829 by Joel R. Poinsett, formerly minister to Mexico.[30] It contained two hundred specimens of minerals, a great quantity of ancient pottery including several hundred representations of human heads and nearly one hundred human figures entire,

[25] *Ibid.*, Jan. 17, 1834, June 18, 1841.
[26] *Ibid.*, Dec. 19, 1803.
[27] *Ibid.*, June 23, 1809.   [28] *Ibid.*, March 20, 1818.
[29] *Ibid.*, May 3, 1805, July 17, 1807.
[30] *Ibid.*, April 2, 1829.

many domestic utensils, musical instruments, and hieroglyphic paintings on paper made of maguey. There were in addition nine stone figures representing human figures in different attitudes, seven masks beautifully worked in alabaster, porphyry, and verd antique, eighteen ceramic masks, "life size but very grotesque," and three alabaster vases. Though less diverse, the gift of W. H. Keating, also made in 1829, supplemented Poinsett's. It contained eleven stone figures representing humans, four masks of the human head, a large quantity of arrow heads, knives, other domestic implements, and many specimens of domestic pottery.[31]

History in another form was represented by the Society's collection of coins and medals. John Vaughan presented in 1801 a lot of coins and medals struck at the Soho Mint near Birmingham; it included ten medallions of such near-contemporary figures as Sir William Howe, Earl Cornwallis, the Kings of Sweden and Naples, Lafayette, and Marie Antoinette.[32] Nicholai Heinrich Weinweck of the Royal Society of Heraldry and Genealogy of Denmark in 1805 presented to Thomas Jefferson a collection of 150 Roman coins from the reign of Augustus to that of Theodosius. Jefferson, as was his practice in such cases, placed the collection in the Philosophical Society, where it was augmented by other gifts of Roman coins from Peter S. du Ponceau in 1817 and the Southwark Library Company in 1852.[33] The Society often received single pieces of coinage, ancient and modern. General Kosciuszko presented a Swedish coin in 1797, and his companion Julian U. Niemcewicz gave a Polish gold one at the same time. The medals were especially varied. William Short sent from Paris in 1824 "the first impressions" of a few of those ordered by Congress to commemorate battles and

---

[31] *Ibid.*, April 2, 1829, May 6, 1831.

[32] "List of Specimens of Coins & Materials, Struck at the Soho Mint," May 15, 1801, Curators' Material, 1801–97.

[33] Jefferson to Caspar Wistar, April 30, 1805, Archives; APS Minutes, July 19, 1805, March 7, 1817, May 21, 1852.

heroes of the Revolution.[34] Joseph Sansom, the Philadelphia artist, gave a number of medals which had interested him as a silhouettist. The last gift the Reverend Dr. Nicholas Collin made to the Society was a gold medallion struck in honor of his fellow countryman Linnaeus which had been presented to Collin by the Swedish Academy of Science.[35] After 1850 the coin collection ceased to grow, though medals of various sorts continued to arrive at the Society for half a century thereafter. Among the last items of currency the Society received were several hundred pieces of trade currency, which had circulated usefully though illicitly in the North during the American Civil War.

History on another level was represented by miscellaneous mementoes of the great. Doubtless the Society's link with Franklin and other founders of the Republic and its proximity to Independence Hall led some donors to select it as a depository for such articles. A box made of wood from Penn's Treaty Elm, a fragment of Plymouth Rock, a stick of wood from the Letitia Penn house, a piece of the works of the clock of Independence Hall, a square of marble from the Capitol "conflagrated" by the British in 1814 were doubtless expected to inspire reverent thoughts and patriotic impulses in those who held or beheld them. More impressive than these scraps were two pieces of furniture. One was the chair with a writing arm on which Jefferson was said to have composed the Declaration of Independence; he took it from Philadelphia to Monticello; his daughter took it to Washington; and when she left that city, she gave the chair to J. Kintzing Kane, of Philadelphia, for the Society. The other chair had been used by members of the Continental Congress and was the gift of Francis Hopkinson's grandson in 1837; it was deposited in the State House in 1872. Two locks of Washington's hair—to which was added many years

[34] William Short to John Vaughan, Oct. 20, 1824, Curators' Material, 1801–97.

[35] Nicholas Collin to John Vaughan, June 28, 1831, *ibid.*

later one of General Jackson's—gave a sense of personal immediacy to these historic remains.

Franklin memorabilia, of course, found special consideration at the Society. In 1792 Richard Bache, the doctor's son-in-law, presented the chair in which Franklin sat when presiding at meetings of the Society held in his house after his return from France in 1785. Joseph Hopkinson, the Signer's son, gave an electric battery said to have belonged to the great man, and Miss Sarah Shewell presented the copper point of a lightning rod thought to have been erected by Franklin's fellow investigator Ebenezer Kinnersley and to have been the first in Philadelphia to be struck with lightning. In 1841 John B. Murray of Liverpool offered the Society the very printing press on which Franklin worked as a journeyman in London on condition that the Society make a donation to the Printers' Pension Society of London. When the Society declined the gift on those terms, Murray sent the press as his personal gift without condition; and Adam Ramage put it in working order so that members might have the satisfaction of pulling a sheet on it.[36]

Two other contributions to the cabinet deserve mention, though they have nothing in common except their Scottish origin. In 1795 the Earl of Buchan, a great admirer of America and Americans, presented a writing box made of yew, with a picture of Galileo laid in the top cover and one of John Napier, the inventor of logarithms, mounted on the inside of the lid. Buchan's wish was that the box should be used by the presidents of the Society in succession. David Rittenhouse did use it; it was returned to the Society after his death, but then apparently it was lost to sight for nearly a century until Henry Phillips, Jr., the Society's librarian, found it in the attic in 1885 and told its story.[37] Buch-

[36] APS Minutes, Oct. 1, Dec. 17, 1841, Feb. 18, 1842.
[37] APS *Proceedings*, XXII (1885), 277–78; *A Catalogue of Portraits and Other Works of Art in the Possession of the American Philosophical Society* (Philadelphia, 1961), 12–13.

an's box has not been used by any president of the Society for some years past.

The other exhibit was a cannon ball said to have been fired at Mary, Queen of Scots, and Douglas when they were escaping from Lochleven Castle in 1568. The donor, William H. Robertson, related the story in a letter to John Vaughan:

We visited the lake last Summer a Year. On arrival at the place of Embarkation on the Border of the Lake near the Fishermen's Huts, we were detained some time in Consequence of the absence of the Boats Fishing. The Old Fisherman, the head Man, after making Signals for the Boats, came to our Carriage & soon found out that we were Americans & very much Interested in every thing connected with the History & life of Sir Walter Scott. He then related the following Anecdote, connected with this Ball: Some 11 or 12 years previous, Sir Walter visited Loch Leven, and was taken to the Island, for the purpose of Examining the Ruins, by the said fisherman, where they spent the Day together, in the course of which while Sitting on the Walls of the Ruins, looking a little to the right of the village of Kinloch [Kinross], Sir Walter points to the point of Land, where Mary landed, & remarks, from such a point were fired 23 Balls which must have struck at such a Distance from the shore, and about which time the Keys of the Castle were thrown overboard. Five or 6 years after this Period, the Owners of the Borders of the Lake decided it was occupying too much Valuable Land, and agreed to reduce its size, by Draining & reducing the Water. The said old Fisherman recollecting the Observation of Sir Walter, 5 or 6 Years previous, takes advantage of the reduced state of the Lake with all his Gang of men, proceeded to the point directed by Sir Walter as the place of Landing; from thence waded in the water taking the Direction of the Castle, when they found 22 of the 23 Balls said to be fired, & also the Keys of the Castle. 21 of the said Balls with the Keys of the Castle are now deposited with the Antiquarian Society in Edinburgh & the 22d is now in your possession.[38]

[38] William H. Robertson to John Vaughan, Oct. 6, 1837, Miscellaneous MSS. The "Old Fisherman" enlarged upon his story, as fishermen are known to have done. The cannon balls are more

4. Tea gathered at Dorchester Neck after the Boston Tea Party, preserved in the American Antiquarian Society.

5. A female mummy taken from the "Mammoth Cave" in Kentucky in October 1815 by Nahum Ward of Marietta, Ohio, and formerly in the cabinet of the American Antiquarian Society. It is now in the Smithsonian Institution.

The cannon ball was deposited in the Historical Society of Pennsylvania in 1874, but was returned to the Society in 1898.

In addition to such relics as these, two other kinds of historical materials were preserved in the cabinet of the Society in the late eighteenth and nineteenth centuries. The more important at the time were the portraits, busts, and engravings, principally of members, which were presented to the Society or, occasionally, purchased by it.[39] Charles Willson Peale in 1785 offered the copy of Martin's portrait of Franklin which he had made some years before; it was the first in the gallery of presidential portraits, which, after 1830, was kept up[40]—Rittenhouse by Peale, Jefferson and Wistar by Sully, Patterson by Rembrandt Peale. In 1803 the Society purchased a portrait of Washington from Gilbert Stuart; today it is the only Stuart Washington in possession of the original purchaser. In the 1820's and 1830's a number of works of art came in—portraits of benefactors such as Joel Poinsett, Alexander Wilson, and John Heckewelder; busts of Nathaniel Chapman, Baron Cuvier, and Simeon DeWitt, surveyor general of New York; a sepia drawing of Zaccheus Collins, long an officer of the Society. In 1823, "on consideration of his extraordinary care and attention to the library, for his great exertions in procuring contributions for it and for his own, very liberal donations," the Society took the unusual step of asking John Vaughan to sit to Sully. All these works of art came under the jurisdiction of the curators. They appear to have been well cared for, especially in the latter part of the century, for the minutes of the Society and reports of the cura-

---

likely to have been fired during a siege of the castle. See R. Burns-Begg, *History of Lochleven Castle* (3rd ed., Kinross, 1887), 24–25; Society of Antiquaries of Scotland, *Proceedings*, III (1857–60), 365. I am indebted to Mr. Stuart Maxwell, of the National Museum of Antiquities of Scotland, for these references.

[39] The fullest account of this topic may be found in the *Catalogue of Portraits and Other Works of Art.*

[40] APS Minutes, July 16, 1830.

tors contain frequent references to cleaning, glazing, labeling, and proper hanging; and they came to be highly valued as a personal record of the Society's history.[41]

The other sort of historical materials in the cabinet were manuscripts, especially any that were sufficiently significant and dramatic to exhibit. The first such "historical" manuscript the Society received was the original Charter of Privileges issued by William Penn in 1701; it was presented to the Society in 1812. In 1825 the grandson of Richard Henry Lee gave a large lot of the latter's papers, including a draft of the Declaration of Independence in Jefferson's hand. Understandably enough, this became one of the Society's principal treasures, shown to visitors with some flourish and only rarely permitted to go elsewhere on exhibition, as to Independence Hall for the observance of the nation's centennial in 1876.[42] Six ancient Aztec manuscripts, four of them leaves from the Tribute Roll of Montezuma, formed part of the Poinsett collection. They were reclaimed from the Academy of Natural Sciences in 1884 and after careful study were reproduced in facsimile in color and published in 1892 with commen-

---

[41] Until 1934 the Society rented parts of its Hall to individuals, such as Peale and Sully, and to institutions, which decorated their rooms with busts and portraits. Some intermingling inevitably followed. In 1899 "amongst old papers &c." in the library an unfinished portrait of Benjamin Rush by Sully was found, presumably left behind when the painter gave up his rooms. The statues of two Roman matrons were stowed away in the attic for many years; they were recognized in 1961 as property of the Athenaeum and one identified as Minerva, and then returned to their former and rightful owners. Still unsolved is the mystery of the Duke of Wellington. His Grace had no connection whatever with the Philosophical Society, and the minutes and curators' records do not mention his bust (*Athenaeum Annals*, VII [1961], No. 9, pp. 1–2). Possibly, like the Roman ladies, he was formerly a guest of the Athenaeum. If so, he could be returned and, with a kind of logic, be placed in the Athenaeum's Bonaparte Room.

[42] I. Minis Hays, "A Note on the History of the Jefferson Manuscript Draught of the Declaration of Independence," APS *Proceedings*, XXXVII (1898), 88–107.

taries by Daniel G. Brinton and others; in 1942 they were returned to Mexico.[43] Though the curators claimed control of such single outstanding items as these, and even once disputed with the librarian the custody of some old papers found in his desk,[44] all manuscripts eventually came directly within the charge of the library, with whose history in the twentieth century theirs is bound up.

The cabinet of the Philosophical Society at the middle of the nineteenth century thus contained a large, highly miscellaneous assortment of natural and artificial curiosities, historical documents and relics, portraits, coins and medals, as well as some articles which defied rational classification, such as the model of Mont Blanc and the girdle of a Berber female. In the words of one of the curators who commented on the history of the collection in 1897, "In not a few instances the donors appear to have acted upon the principle that any item possessing sufficient novelty, even if not of much scientific value, should find its proper resting place in the Cabinet of the Philosophical Society,—and the Society received the same, with thanks."[45] Inevitably the Society's museum appeared to many visitors to be only a meaningless and useless clutter. James Silk Buckingham, an English traveler who was hospitably received at Philosophical Hall and warmly praised the Mexican and Peruvian collections, expressed the judgment that, with the exception of Peale's, museums in the United States were "in general so full of worthless and trashy articles" as to be hardly worth a visit.[46]

---

[43] APS Minutes, Jan. 4, Feb. 1, 1884; Daniel G. Brinton and others, "The Tribute Roll of Montezuma," APS *Transactions*, New Ser., XVII (1893), 53–61; APS *Year Book 1942*, 35–36.

[44] J. Cheston Morris to Edwin J. Houston, Oct. 20, 1899, Archives.

[45] "American Philosophical Society as to the Cabinet," Feb. 22, 1897, Curators' Reports.

[46] *The Eastern and Western States of America* (London, [1842]), I, 539; *America, Historical, Statistic, and Descriptive* (London, [1841]), II, 65. See also Ramon de la Sagra, *Cinq mois aux Etats-Unis* (Brussels, 1837), 89, and Frederick von Raumer, *America and the American People* (New York, 1856), 473.

Captain Marryat's judgment was still harsher: American museums, including those of Philadelphia, which he thought the best in the country, were

> such collections as would be made by schoolboys . . .
> not . . . erudite professors and scientific men. Side by
> side with the most interesting and valuable specimens,
> such as the fossil mammoth, etc., you have the greatest
> puerilities and absurdities in the world—such as a
> cherrystone formed into a basket, a fragment of the
> boiler of the *Moselle* steamer, and Heaven knows what
> besides. Then you invariably have a large collection of
> daubs, called portraits of eminent personages, one-half
> of whom a stranger never heard of.[47]

Marryat had been drinking when he was brought to Philosophical Hall and had rudely refused to look at the collections there;[48] but when he wrote those words he might very well have had in mind the Society's cabinet as well as Peale's Museum and the Franklin Institute.

However, the collections of the Society were being put to modest uses in ways which Marryat and other visitors did not appreciate or even suspect. From time to time, for example, specimens were loaned to individuals for study, as fragments of mastodons were to Dr. Caspar Wistar; while George W. Featherstonhaugh was permitted to borrow mineral and other geological materials in 1831 to illustrate his public lectures.[49] In addition, the paleontological specimens were sometimes reproduced for the use of scholars or for display in institutions at a distance. As early as 1825 the Society authorized casts to be made of the claws of a megalonyx for the Lyceum of Natural History of New York;[50] and in 1831 it directed copies to be made of the excellent casts of mastodon's bones collected by Dr.

[47] Frederick Marryat, *A Diary in America, With Remarks on Its Institutions*, ed. Sydney W. Jackman (New York, 1964), 148.
[48] Samuel Breck, *Recollections*, ed. H. E. Scudder (Philadelphia, 1877), 290–93.
[49] APS Minutes, Feb. 18, 1831. See also Oct. 1, Nov. 5, 1830.
[50] *Ibid.*, Feb. 18, 1825.

Isaac Lea of Philadelphia. Sets were sent to the Jardin des Plantes in Paris, the Geological Society of London, and, a few years later, to the museum in Darmstadt.[51] Still another way in which the collections were made more useful was by exchange. An exchange of duplicate coins was authorized in 1805, and the practice was soon extended to other articles, especially minerals and shells.[52] Finally, exhibits were sometimes loaned for display outside the Hall, so that they were seen by many who did not visit the Society personally. The deposit of the Indian elephant in Peale's Museum is an illustration; and when the Museum was broken up, the elephant was sent to the University, where the Society's mastodon head had already been placed.[53] A unique collection of relics of another kind—Jefferson's draft copy of the Declaration of Independence, the writing chair he used in Philadelphia in 1776, and Sully's portrait of him—were shown in 1847 at a benefit exhibition of the Musical Fund Society of Philadelphia. In 1864 the curators were authorized to lend anything in the Society's cabinet for exhibition at the United States Sanitary Commission Fair in Philadelphia.[54]

Such measures as these, admittedly, did not vastly increase the usefulness of the museum. The collections for the most part remained in the Hall, where few specimens were well arranged or exhibited to good advantage. The fact was that the Hall was too small to house and show the collections properly and that there was no one, not even a curator, with time, interest, and, in many cases, competence to study, arrange, and evaluate the various specimens. By 1840 the museum was demonstrably an old-fashioned eighteenth-century cabinet of undifferentiated curiosities. It could not equal in extent or depth the more specialized collections of

---

[51] *Ibid.*, Dec. 3, 1831, Jan. 20, 1832, March 15, Oct. 4, 1833, April 18, 1834, May 20, 1842.
[52] *Ibid.*, May 3, 1805, Oct. 15, 1830.
[53] *Ibid.*, June 19, 1845.
[54] *Ibid.*, Nov. 5, 1847; APS *Proceedings*, IX (1864), 349.

other institutions, and with few exceptions—notably the Mexican antiquities—its holdings were equaled and excelled elsewhere. Nathan Dunn's Chinese Museum, for example, was unrivaled in its field in Philadelphia.[55] Dr. Lea had an incomparable private collection of shells and minerals—Marryat thought it the most interesting museum of the kind he saw in America and spent two days examining it.[56] Even the Athenaeum of Philadelphia, basically a reading room and subscription library, aspired to collections of coins and minerals. But by far the most important of the specialized scientific institutions in Philadelphia was the Academy of Natural Sciences. Founded in 1812, it had long been a center for research and publication in biology, zoology, botany, and their related sciences; and it had a large, well-arranged museum. Between it and the Philosophical Society were many personal ties, for several men, notably Franklin Peale and Joseph Leidy, were active in both institutions.

In 1849 the Philosophical Society took a decision which proved to be the first step toward the policy which led to the eventual dispersal of its collections. In that year the curators were authorized to deposit in the Academy of Natural Sciences the fossil organic remains in the Society's cabinet, on condition that the Academy agree to take proper measures to preserve the specimens and return them if called for.[57] These terms were readily accepted, and they became the for-

[55] On Dunn's Chinese Museum, see Buckingham, *Eastern and Western States*, II, 42–73, and George Combe, *Notes on the United States of North America, during a Phrenological Visit in 1838–39–40* (Edinburgh, 1841), I, 3067.
The Society's museum lost some of its unique and preeminent character as similar museums were established in the neighboring county towns of Pennsylvania. The Chester County Cabinet of Natural Sciences was founded in 1826, and the Bucks and Montgomery County Cabinets five years later. See Hazard's *Register of Pennsylvania*, I (1828), 302–4, VIII (1831), 1–2, IX (1832), 116–18.
[56] Marryat, *Diary in America*, 147.
[57] APS Minutes, Nov. 2, 1849.

mula for subsequent deposits. The Society's action of 1849 was followed by deposits of additional similar materials in 1852 and 1860. In 1863 "the admirable Herbarium" of Dr. Charles W. Short, one of several he had presented to the Society, was placed in the Academy.[58]

One result of these deposits was to leave more space in Philosophical Hall for the remaining collections. There was a flurry of awakened interest in the cabinet in the 1850's. One member offered to arrange the coins and medals. The curators were directed to collect apparatus and specimens which had been loaned but not returned and to prepare a catalogue of the collections. In 1853 the Society authorized the exchange of duplicate coins, medals, minerals, and other specimens for articles of equal value which would be significant additions to its own collections.[59]

The policy of dispersal which had begun in 1849 received more precise definition in 1864. In that year, at the instigation of Dr. Joseph Leidy, its curator, who was also a member of the Philosophical Society, the Academy of Natural Sciences proposed to deposit in the Society's cabinet all its specimens of "antique art." The ostensible reason was to facilitate the study of archaeology by concentrating materials in the Society's museum; the real purpose of the Academy's action was to promote an exchange which would bring to the Academy the Society's natural history collections. No hint of this purpose appeared in Leidy's letter to the Society. "With the rich nucleus possessed by the latter," he explained, "I hope soon to see a noble Archaeological Museum, which will be one of the scientific attractions of our city."[60]

This offer resulted in a thoughtful reappraisal by the curators of the Society's cabinet. Regardless of any

[58] *Ibid.*, April 16, 1852, April 6, 1860, Dec. 18, 1863.
[59] *Ibid.*, Nov. 21, 1851, May 6, 1853.
[60] Joseph Leidy to J. P. Lesley, Feb. 23, 1864, Curators' Material, 1801–97.

benefits to archaeological studies, it was clear to the
curators that the deposit of the Society's natural history collections at the Academy would promote useful
knowledge directly by making the materials more accessible and indirectly by relieving the desperate over-
crowding in the Hall. Franklin Peale, one of the curators, described conditions there:

Many books are now, of necessity, placed in the
Museum, the cases, however, being entirely unsuited to
their proper accommodation. These cases being sparsely
occupied by the collections of minerals and fossils,
shells, fossils, and minerals are also stowed and packed
in various closets, under cases, in their present condition inaccessible to observer or student, and, therefore,
in no condition to aid the "promotion of knowledge."

Bottles containing specimens in spirits are drying
up, or have entirely evaporated, and a case of insects
contains only the reliquiae of the contents, and has
almost literally turned to the original dust from which
they were created.

With these facts before them, the members of the
Society will be able to appreciate the objects in view,
and to vote understandingly on the resolution offered.

Resolved, That so many of the specimens of the collection of minerals and fossils belonging to the Society,
as the Curators may select, be deposited in the Cabinet
of the Academy of Natural Sciences.[61]

The Society accepted the curators' recommendations,
received the "antique art" from the Academy, and deposited in that institution still more of its own fossil
and mineral specimens.[62] As for the prospect of "a
noble Archaeological Museum" which Leidy had held
out, despite its attractions for a few members of the
Society, nothing was done to establish it; and only a
dozen years later the Society sent the Academy all of
its prehistoric Mexican and Peruvian artifacts which
Poinsett, Keating, and others had collected.[63]

Hardly had the Philosophical Society adopted this

[61] APS *Proceedings,* IX (1864), 354.
[62] APS Minutes, March 18, 1864; Joseph Leidy, Receipt,
March 28, 1864, Curators' Material, 1801–97.
[63] APS Minutes, Nov. 16, 1877, Dec. 6, 1878.

policy when one member proposed that the Society underwrite a systematic approach to Indian ethnology. In 1867 F. V. Hayden, professor of geology in the University of Pennsylvania, who had been a member of exploring parties in the Bad Lands, Black Hills, and other parts of the West, recommended that a photographic record be made of persons and scenery of the trans-Mississippi regions, with special reference to the aborigines. A committee was appointed, a small sum was appropriated, and in 1868 the first album of photographs was received by the Society.[64] But Hayden's project seemed at variance with the Society's museum policy; other agencies, such as the Smithsonian Institution and the Bureau of American Ethnology, already had fuller records of the West; and the Society did nothing more about Hayden's suggestion.

Meanwhile unsolicited gifts and bequests created fresh problems. One of these concerned the Franklin Peale collection of some eighteen hundred implements of the Stone Age, "collected and arranged as impressively confirming the Unity of the human race," which was bequeathed to the Society by his widow in 1875.[65] Peale had often shown pieces of his collection to the Society, describing single specimens and groups of specimens in both informal talks and formal papers.[66] Many members had expected that the Society would receive the collection in Peale's lifetime or at his death and had been disappointed when it did not. Mrs. Peale's will required that the collection be exhibited as a unit, that it be housed in a fireproof building, and that it be accessible to all visitors. Only the first of these stipulations was within the power of the Society to fulfill, for its building was not fireproof and its museum was not normally open to any but its own

[64] *Ibid.*, Feb. 15, 1867, April 3, 1868.

[65] Caroline E. G. Peale, Extract from will, probated Oct. 12, 1875, Curators' Material, 1801–97.

[66] See, for example, Peale's communications between 1861 and 1868 in APS *Proceedings*, VII, 411–15, VIII, 265–72, IX, 401–3, X, 243–44, 430–35.

members. The Society accepted the collection, however, promising to store it in a bank vault, where it would be safe from fire. As this solution hardly met the terms of Mrs. Peale's will, at the suggestion of her executor the collection was deposited in 1877 at the Academy of Natural Sciences.[67]

In line with its now-established policy the Society in 1878 deposited its collection of coins and medals with the Numismatic and Antiquarian Society of Philadelphia, which had been founded in 1855. The Numismatic Society placed the collection on exhibition in Memorial Hall, one of the permanent buildings constructed for the Centennial Exhibition of 1876; and some years later, with the approval of the Philosophical Society, it transferred the collection to the care of the Pennsylvania Museum and School of Industrial Art, which occupied Memorial Hall well into the twentieth century.[68]

In 1890–91 Philosophical Hall was enlarged by the addition of a third floor, and a fireproof vault was constructed. This addition was made principally to provide for the rapidly expanding library, for which the available space was no longer sufficient; but it meant also that the furniture and furnishings of the two rooms on the second floor—the meeting room and the North Room—could be rearranged. To the curators these changes seemed to afford opportunities for exhibiting the collections in the cabinet in more fitting manner.

Dr. J. Cheston Morris had been elected one of the curators in 1889. Energetic, strong-willed, a hard worker, he was reelected to the post each year until 1901, and during these years appears to have been the

[67] W. S. W. Ruschenberger to APS Curators, Oct. 25, 1877; Ruschenberger to J. P. Lesley, Nov. 30, 1878, Curators' Material, 1801–97.

[68] "Catalogue of Coins, Medals &c. belonging to the American Philosophical Society," deposited by the Numismatic and Antiquarian Society in the Pennsylvania Museum and School of Industrial Art, Dec. 19, 1878; F. D. Langenheim to Daniel G. Brinton, April 11, 1895, Curators' Material, 1801–97.

most influential, certainly the most articulate, of the curators, whose chairman he often was. His first action was to propose that the curators examine and arrange all the articles remaining in their charge, and he asked $100 for the inevitable expenses. Predictably the curators found that better accommodations for the collections were desirable, and they proposed that a committee be named to find space.[69] Morris also stimulated the members' interest in the cabinet by exhibiting some of its treasures from time to time.[70] In 1891 the Society recalled the Peale collection from the Academy, and in the next year Morris proposed that all collections on deposit anywhere should be returned to the Society.[71]

Though this proposal undoubtedly appealed to the Society's pride and to some members' sense of history, it was recognized as both impracticable and undesirable. Should the collections be returned to the Hall, they would fill up most of the space which the remodeling had gained for the library. Moreover, it was clear that a modern museum required the attention of a staff of experts, which the Society could not provide. When the opinion was expressed that the Academy had not fully catalogued the prehistoric American collections, Daniel G. Brinton and others connected with the University of Pennsylvania saw an opportunity to get the collection for its department of archaeology and paleontology. In the end, however, the Academy expressed its desire to retain the materials on deposit and the Society concluded that that was where they should stay.[72]

The Society had thus made it clear that it had no

[69] APS Minutes, May 17, 1889, Jan. 17, 1890, Dec. 4, 1891.

[70] Ibid., Dec. 18, 1891, Jan. 1, 1892.

[71] Robert Patterson to Frederick Fraley, Dec. 5, 1890, Curators' Material, 1801–97; APS Minutes, Dec. 4, 1891, March 18, 1892. Patterson, as executor of Mrs. Peale's estate, corresponded with the Society's officers about the Franklin Peale Stone Age Collection. It is an interesting sidelight on institutional sociology that in 1891 the collection was sometimes called the "Patterson collection."

[72] APS Proceedings, XXX (1892), 315–16, XXXI (1893), 5–6, 13, 133; APS Minutes, May 20, 1892; Curators' Special Report, May 6, 1892, Curators' Material, 1801–97.

thought of reversing its long-standing policy of making deposits of museum materials. Morris and his fellow curators accepted the decision and turned their energies toward preserving and organizing what was left. They vigorously protested against careless handling of collections by the Committee on Library, asking the Society to direct that "no radical change should be made in the arrangement of the articles in our care without our approval and under our supervision."[73] They sent more articles of natural history, notably the botanical collections of Lewis and Clark and Muhlenberg, to the Academy; to the Wagner Free Institute of Science in Philadelphia they sent a quantity of rocks and minerals found in the basement; and they added to the deposit in the Pennsylvania Museum coins and medals received during the preceding twenty years.[74] They had an abstract made of all the Society's actions on the cabinet since 1769, and wherever possible a notation was added of the present whereabouts of each article.[75] In 1897 Morris reported:

The Cabinet at present contains what might be called the residuum left by much good work done in the past, together with certain articles of historic value, chiefly from association with Members of the Society.

It also gives space to some objects which no doubt *were* of passing interest at the time they were deposited, but have long since become useless, in fact comparatively uninteresting from any point of view.[76]

[73] "Curators' Report on Damage to the Museum Collections," April 14, 1893, Curators' Reports.

[74] "I rolled up my sleeves yesterday," Thomas Meehan of the Academy wrote Morris gratefully on Aug. 13, 1897, "and spent the whole day, in going through Barton's Herbarium, and just as I was about giving up, I found in the last lot I handled, the package of Lewis & Clarke referred to in the Society's Minutes. . . . You have in the cause of botanical Science builded better than you knew, or I anticipated, in turning these plants over to us."

[75] These abstracts, which fill four volumes, are labeled "Curators Record. Donations." They have proved an invaluable guide to materials for this study.

[76] "American Philosophical Society as to the Cabinet," Feb. 22, 1897, Curators' Reports.

These articles of historic value were now Morris' special concern. He felt that they should be properly arranged and exhibited in the same room with the Society's publications, which, he said, were the Society's principal work and achievement. With this intention, however, he came into conflict again with the Committees on Library and Hall. Morris wanted the North Room fitted up for the remaining collections; but the Society resolved that the library should have it, although the Peale Collection was allowed to stay there.[77] He wanted to place a few of the larger paleontological specimens in the meeting room; but in this he was opposed by the chairman of the Committee on Hall, J. Sergeant Price, a lawyer, as strong-willed and imperious as he. "The committee on Hall will not approve of placing the plaster cast of your headless monster above the door in the Hall," he told Morris peremptorily. Morris docketed the letter, possibly in speechless indignation, simply "Headless."[78]

After 1897 there was little work for the curators to do. Practically all of the museum holdings that had any scientific or educational value had been deposited in other institutions; the rest, such as rocks separated from their labels and butterflies crumbled into dust, was thrown out. Only some larger astronomical and mathematical instruments, some early models of machinery, and the portraits remained. From time to time the curators inspected the deposits in other institutions or reported on the condition of the paintings and sculpture in the Hall.[79] Once in a while, as on the occasion of the Jamestown Exposition of 1907, they had to con-

[77] APS Minutes, April 2, 1897.
[78] J. Sergeant Price to J. Cheston Morris, Dec. 17, 1896, Curators' Material (Not Catalogued [1964]). On another occasion Price threatened to have the janitor remove from the Hall specimens Morris had used to illustrate a lecture if Morris did not remove them himself within the week. Price to Morris, April 29 [1897?], Curators' Material (Not Catalogued [1964]).
[79] Curators' Report, Dec. 6, 1901, Curators' Reports; APS Minutes, May 5, 1893, May 8, 1897.

sider a request to lend the Franklin chair or the Jefferson draft of the Declaration or another relic.[80] Rarely any more did the Society receive a gift, although a suit of fifteenth-century Persian armor, "richly ornamented in damascene," came in in 1915. By the end of the century the history of the Society's cabinet had come to an end—or might be thought to have come to a close but for two things.

In the 1920's the curators several times made the sensible proposal that the deposits should be converted into gifts. Dr. I. Minis Hays, the librarian, objected for reasons that do not appear, and no action was taken.[81] As a result, the deposits remained deposits still, subject to the Society's recall. Although the recipients have no reason to expect that they will ever be asked to give them up, the Society did exercise its right in 1930, when it recalled the Poinsett collection from the Academy of Natural Sciences and placed it in the University Museum.[82] And since the deposits remain deposits, there is also the possibility that the depositories may send back what they do not want. This happened in 1952 when the Philadelphia Museum of Art, as successor to the Pennsylvania Museum and School of Industrial Art, returned the coin collection that had been so long in Memorial Hall.[83] And, of course, there is nothing to

[80] William Shields McKean to Edgar Fahs Smith, March 23, 1907, Curators' Material, 1900–1963.

[81] Curators' Report, Jan. 20, 1922, Jan. 20, 1923; I. Minis Hays to Council, Jan. 23, 1923, Curators' Reports.

[82] APS *Proceedings*, LXIX (1930), xvii–xviii.

[83] Philadelphia Museum, Receipt, June 23, 1952, Curators' Material, 1900–1963.

The practice of deposits may operate another way. In 1883 the Moravian Church asked for the return of Indian missionary manuscripts which they had deposited in the APS many years before. Because Bishop de Schweinitz' letterhead of 1883 gave an official name to the church different from that recorded by the Society, the latter's officers demanded proof of succession. The Moravians provided it in ample form, in a letter which did not conceal their impatience with such lawyerly nit-picking. In 1962 another institution asked for the return of manuscripts which the APS had catalogued, repaired, and preserved for 30 years; but they were satisfied with a microfilm.

prevent someone from bequeathing or presenting to the Society anything significant, interesting, or merely strange. Thus in 1959 a model of the sloop of war *Peacock*, one of the vessels of the United States Exploring Expedition of Lieutenant Charles Wilkes, was given to the Society and, it may be added, gratefully received, for it made a handsome addition to the decoration of the library.

In 1967, more than a century after the policy of deposit was adopted, only scattered fragments remain. Some larger scientific instruments and a few mechanical models have been repaired, placed on view, and described in a printed catalogue.[84] A bunch of spears and arrows in a corner of the basement of the library is all that remains of the Society's once-great Indian collection; while classical archaeology is represented by the beautiful Etruscan kylix which Joseph Bonaparte presented in 1836 and an "Etruscan lamp" which Mrs. L. E. S. Peale picked up at Herculaneum in 1830. No bones of mastodons or megalonyx, no headed or beheaded monsters, no crumbling plaster casts remind the twentieth-century visitor of the extensive paleontological collection which the Hall once held. The coin collection, rejected by the Philadelphia Museum of Art, lies unnoticed and untended in the attic.[85]

If at the close of the second century of the Society's existence, its cabinet no longer functions as a museum, two other categories of material that once were part of the cabinet still contribute to the Society's work. The portraits and prints remain, a few of superior quality; and so do the manuscripts, including the Jefferson draft of the Declaration of Independence. Though not on exhibition, this may still be considered one of the sights of Philadelphia, with the State House, Fairmount Park, and the newly-scrubbed City Hall. Of the

[84] Multhauf, *Catalogue of Instruments and Models.*
[85] Or did until May 1967, when, having been examined by experts and found to be of little value for scholarly purposes or financially, it was sold for the library's benefit.

Society's cabinet in its present form as in its heyday one might say what J. Cheston Morris said of it in 1897:

It illustrated in some degree the diversification which already began to characterize the progress of the New States. It testified to the fact that the Philosophical Society occupied a responsive and favorable position in relation to *all* branches of systematized research, as its founder intended. From this point of view the Cabinet became a potent means in fulfilling the purpose for which the Society was founded.[86]

[86] "American Philosophical Society as to the Cabinet," Feb. 22, 1897.

The Museum of
the American Antiquarian
Society

Clifford K. Shipton

IN 1909 the American Antiquarian Society was forced by the need to construct a new building to face up to the fact, which had been struggling for attention for almost a century, that it could not be effective both as a museum and as a research library. Its long history as a museum which was on its death-bed for fifty years is instructive and faintly amusing; often I visit historical society museums in which I can measure the degree of *rigor mortis* by the experience of my own Society.

The first decade of the nineteenth century was marked by a great wave of proud nationalism of which an interest in our history and prehistory was a part. This interest was combined with the popular scientific curiosity which had marked the intellectual revival of the eighteenth century. One of its manifestations, the cabinet of curiosities kept by every true virtuoso, contained all kinds of objects which chanced to interest him, or gave him an opportunity to crow over his rival collectors. In the early nineteenth century there had come upon the scene the popular museum, which contained anything which might interest the common man sufficiently to induce him to pay an admission fee. Another variety, the museum at Harvard College, typical of those maintained by institutions, was described in 1783 as a room or cabinet of natural history" which hardly deserves the name," consisting of a few things "placed there in a disorderly manner."[1]

[1] This and all subsequent quoted statements are derived from the archives of the American Antiquarian Society.

This was the prevailing situation of the museum in America when in 1812 a group of New Englanders "influenced by a desire to contribute," they said, "to the advancement of the Arts and Sciences . . . by . . . collecting, and preserving such materials as may be useful in making their progress . . . and . . . to assist the researchers of the future historians of our country," requested the Commonwealth of Massachusetts to incorporate them as the American Antiquarian Society, pointing out that there was then "no public association for such purposes in the United States." Of their proposed corporation, they said: "Its immediate and peculiar design is to discover the antiquities of Our Continent, and by providing a fixed, and permanent place of deposit, to preserve such relics of American Antiquity as are portable, as well as to collect and preserve those of other parts of the Globe." They already had, they said, a valuable collection of books, "some of them more ancient than are to be found in any other part of our country," and they proposed to collect "fossils, handicrafts of the Aborigines, &c." For these they would build a library and museum in Worcester, Massachusetts, which was described as a "safe inland town [this was in 1812] on the great roads west and south."

At the first annual meeting of the American Antiquarian Society, William Jenks, in his official address, thought it necessary to justify its anthropological interests by arguing that research on the Indians might prove their connection with Noah. There was no question but that this research would be pushed as far as possible in literary sources, for President Isaiah Thomas had made his name as a publisher, had written the standard history of American printing, and was interested almost entirely in bibliography and book collecting. Still, the librarian and cabinet keeper was ordered to catalogue and price all objects, other than books, in the possession of the Society.

The announcement of the program of American Antiquarian Society struck a chord which sounded in every corner of the country. Soon letters were received asking where antiquities destined for its cabinet should be sent. First, a place of temporary deposit was designated at Boston; and later, receiving officers were appointed in all the chief cities in the country. Many members were elected with an eye to their performance of this service. They were frankly told that their membership was not honorary in the sense that it relieved them from the obligation of collecting for the Society. Timothy Alden, who was immensely interested in this aspect of its work, proposed that each receiving officer be given the title of librarian of the Society for the city in which he worked, and he nominated DeWitt Clinton as librarian for New York. That turned out to be a good choice, for Clinton's net fell wide and brought into the Society such diverse things as the Alabama Stone and the Celeron plate from the Ohio. Other receivers were diligent, if less spectacular, in their achievements. The first receiver appointed for Portland advertised in the newspapers for antiquities and prepared a place of deposit for them. One of the first of the objects contributed was an ax of French manufacture which had been discovered six feet below the surface, and beside it "a *toad*, in a state of motionless insensibility, but which recovered activity after about an hour's exposure to the air." He sent the ax, but not the toad, to Worcester.

The first page of the accession list of the cabinet keeper gives a glimpse of the museum as of 1813:

Chinese pass for the Ship John Jay of Providence, which pass cost at Canton 500 dollars.
Two small pieces of Palm Leaf, on which are several lines written with a Stilus, in the Malayan Language.
Forty pieces of Silver Coin [not associated with Judas].
A lady's Silver Trinkett, made in the year 1111, or 1121, consisting of a Tooth, Ear, and Nail Picker.
The identical Whetstone owned by Dr. Increase Mather . . . used by him to whet the knife with which he made

his Pens whilst President . . . likewise used by his son Dr. Cotton Mather when he wrote the *Magnalia*.

In 1817 the system of regional receivers was replaced by geographical representation on the Council of the Society, for the problem had already become that of handling the flow of material. Caleb Atwater wrote from Circleville, Ohio, that he was daily acquiring Indian antiquities which he would send to Worcester. By 1819 the Society was sending a form letter to contributors asking that artifacts sent in "be accompanied with some account of the place of their deposit, probable age, supposed use, and any other matter" which might "elucidate their history."

The most famous of the early acquisitions of the Society was the "Mammoth Cave Mummy" discovered in 1816 and taken to Lexington, Kentucky, where it became "the subject of great curiosity," But, "being much exposed to the atmosphere, it gradually began to decay; its muscles to contract, and the teeth to drop out, and much of its hair was plucked from its head by wanton visitants." The owner therefore gave it to one Nahum Ward, to deliver to the Society, but he appropriated it to his own use, which was to travel around the country with it and exhibit it for a fee. The Society finally recovered the mummy and gave it a seat of honor in its museum, where it attracted the unfavorable comments of President Thomas:

Very few persons attend to see the skeleton; as those who do, universally express their disgust at it. For myself, I cannot perceive how the cause of science, history or antiquarianism is to be benefitted by the preservation of those dried up particles. I have seen a dead cat, which accidentally was inclosed in an oven, and found some months afterwards, in as good a state of mummy preservation as this skeleton. The best thing in my opinion which could be done with it would be to give it to some anatomical school or bury it in the cemetery.

Quite another fate was in store for this Indian lady, however, for she was a part of the Society's exhibition in the World's Fairs of 1876 and 1893, and finally came to rest in the Smithsonian Institution.

In response to calls for a "catalogue of the cabinet," so that donors might see what was needed, one was printed in 1819. The completion of the first Antiquarian Hall in the next year raised the problem of service, which for the time being was provided by having the Worcester members keep the library and cabinet open one day a week, serving in rotation. In this period some visitors enjoyed guides who were very prominent political and judicial figures. After two years this system proved to be too much of a burden, so it was voted to close the cabinet until further notice and to open the library "to none but literary characters." In 1825 a committee appointed to arrange the cabinet found the task too great, so the following year the librarian was instructed to engage an individual to put the library and cabinet in order; his fortunate choice fell upon Christopher Columbus Baldwin. Three months later it was reported that the cabinet was in order and that every stranger who had "procured the permission of a member of the Society for his admission" had "freely visited the Halls and viewed the rich and rare deposits contained there."

During Baldwin's administration the library was open from nine A.M. to one P.M. (ten A.M. to one P.M. in winter) and from three to five P.M., although there could have been few winter visitors, for fire and lights were forbidden except in the librarian's office. The cabinet was open from eleven A.M. to twelve noon to those visitors who came with a personal introduction or a ticket by a member of the Society. In 1833 this was regarded as a generous policy, for the Society reported that "In accordance with the liberal views of the great benefactor of the Institution, the collections have been open to the public under certain necessary regulations and have been occasionally resorted to by the strangers from all parts of the Union." It is perhaps as well that there were not more visitors, for Baldwin remarked that he talked for three days with one man who interested him. After Baldwin's administration the rules were liberalized to admit to the cabinet, during the hour that it was open, visitors "whether attracted by curiosity or in pursuit of information." Estimates of the quality of the collection differed according to the interests of the visitors. The Duke of Saxe-Weimar-Eisenach in 1825 complained that the museum was in its infancy and contained but few interesting specimens; but the cabinet keeper insisted that the "collection of the weapons of Indian warfare, ornaments of savage dress and vessels of culinary use [was] probably unrivalled for extent and variety."

The variety of the collections was increased in 1825 when the Worcester Lyceum of National History deposited its collections in Antiquarian Hall, and again ten years later when the Worcester Athenaeum did the same. Both of these organizations became extinct, but in 1854 their functions were taken over by another, and their possessions withdrawn to become the nucleus of a new Museum of Natural History. The American Antiquarian Society was always loath to get into the natural history field, and in 1832 it was very dubious about accepting a collection of marine shells. Baldwin personally collected insects—intentionally and for purposes of study, that is—but he passed his specimens along to the cabinet of Harvard College.

When Aaron Bancroft was going to Ohio in 1832, Baldwin told him, "What I particularly want and am desirous of procuring is a collection of skulls. I want the skulls of the unknown forgotten people who built the mounds and forts." His mail had for sometime been running to letters inquiring about Indian skulls. A visit to the museum of the New-York Historical Society in 1833 led him to enumerate his principles:

There were very few objects of curiosity or antiquity in the collection. This is correct taste. A library should contain nothing but books, coins, statuary and pictures. I admit now and then that an antiquity should be admitted. But how absurd to pile up old bureaus and chests, and stuff them with old coats and hats and high-heeled shoes. The true history of all these things are handed down by painting. And besides, if they are once received there will be attempts making to fool somebody with the "Shield of Achilles." . . . I have discouraged the sending them to the Antiquarian Hall for this reason.

The point was reasonable. The American Antiquarian Society had been the foremost organization in the field now known as anthropology, and it did well to specialize there. Baldwin was killed in 1835 when his stagecoach upset in Ohio while he was on his way out to open Indian mounds. His successor's first instructions were "to make the aboriginal remains of this continent a matter of personal research and study." Samuel Foster Haven, who became librarian in 1838, did become one of the nation's leading anthropologists.

Haven took over a museum which was impressive by the standards of the day:

The Cabinet occupies one large room, and has been arranged with great neatness. Beside an extensive collection of foreign and native minerals, and of shells, many of them of singular beauty and high scientific value, but not peculiarly appropriate to the objects of the institution, there are old specimens of the arts of Peru and Mexico; a vast number of implements, utensils, weapons, and ornaments of the northern Indians, and some most interesting memorials of the planters of New England, and the patriots of the revolution. The coins exceed two thousand in number; some hundreds bear the impress of the emperors of Rome; there are many stamped with the pine tree of the province and the Indian of the Commonwealth of Massachusetts; and most of those which have been issued in the several American States are preserved.

Haven soon transferred to better hands the inappropriate natural history material, but he classified the coins and published a report on the American pieces. His record of his museum activities is not as full as a historian would wish; one wonders at his report that he had received "an ancient collection of Unheard of Curiosities." As a matter of fact, he did not have the ability which a good museum man, like a good woman, should have of saying "No." Nor did he have any concept of service to the public. He referred to visitors as "a crowd of careless people . . . regardless of admonition, and intent only on the gratification of curiosity." All that he could do with them, he said, was to watch their ingress and egress, "and give them cautions and trust to their sense of propriety." The Society was, he contended, "intended for scientific use and gratification of enlightened curiosity" and was not "a mere museum of articles for idle and unprofitable inspection." It is curious to find him complaining in 1842 that fashion had taken up antiquity, so that "old pictures, old furniture, old Plate" were "now sought with eagerness as necessary adjuncts of style and the most cherished ornaments of the drawing room." His Council, however, told him not to be worried by this competition: "Properly speaking, our country offers but one legitimate field for the investigations of the antiquary. All, except its aboriginal history, is too modern for mystery, and almost too modern for obscurity or doubt."

In 1850, when making an appropriation for the exploration of the Indian mounds of Wisconsin, the Council of the Society officially recognized the fact that it was unable to cope with the whole field of American anthropology. Its solution was to recommend that Congress provide that historical surveys be made by surveying parties, like that which was to run the boundary between Texas and Mexico. The next year the Society turned over to the Smithsonian Institution for publication the results of its Wisconsin exploration. The scheme for the organization of the Smithsonian had been submitted to the Council of the American Antiquarian Society for comment and criticism, and active cooperation between the two institutions was the rule. Secretary Joseph Henry of the Smithsonian was an active member of the American Antiquarian Society. In 1855 its Council described the Washington museum as "the metropolitan institution of the country, possessing peculiar advantages, not only from its connection with the government, but by its ample means." For a time there was some uncertainty of sphere, the Society withdrawing from large bibliographical projects in which the Smithsonian had expressed an interest; but the division was fairly clear by 1860, when the United States National Museum turned its newspaper collection over to the Society.

An opportunity for a change in collecting policy presented itself to the Society with the completion of a new building in 1853. The old structure, a handsome Georgian building of typical New England frame and clapboard construction, had fallen into hopeless decay within thirty years of its opening. This deterioration was blamed on the forest of trees which Christopher Columbus Baldwin had planted around it with his own hand, trees which added to the natural dampness of the site.

The librarian, Haven, probably designed the heating for the new building for it kept his office at 80°, while the temperature in the book stacks was 40°, and in the museum, 20°. It had been the intention of the architects to put the museum in the rather cramped quarters of the lower hall, while designing the more desirable upper hall for a reading room and book stacks. This division was soon disrupted by President Salisbury's determination to enlarge the art museum function of the Society. In 1858 he had made and brought to America a handsome and competent plaster cast of Michelangelo's huge statue of Christ leaning on the cross. The members of the Society found it installed in the reading room when they met there for the annual meeting. Councilor Barton's remark that he "was taken by surprise" was typical of the reaction although one fluent gentlemen said: "I have rarely been impressed with a stronger emotion of astonishment and awe, than when, as I entered this room this morning, the first object which met my view was this beautiful and impressive statue." Haven, troubled by this invasion of his book area, made a frantic effort to draw the statue into the Americana field by pointing out that the Society in its early days had held its meetings on the anniversary of the Landing of Columbus, and that Christopher meant Christ Bearer: "If, at the foundation of this Society, the shade of the exalted navigator could have been evoked, and besought for an emblem that should embody and express the proper spirit of American History, we may believe that he would have pointed to the work of his great contemporary . . . and have exclaimed, 'There is the emblem of my mission.' "

If, some of the members reasoned, there were to be statues in the Hall, then certainly Isaiah Thomas, the founder of the Society, should be represented; before long a likeness of him stood beside the work of Michelangelo. This was soon joined by another heroic plaster cast presented by Mr. Salisbury, a really good reproduction of Michelangelo's Moses. One can, however, detect the president's doubts of the appropriateness of his gift by his too prominent argument that Moses belonged there because he was a historian. The Council of the Society very definitely resisted this trend into the art museum field: "We cannot suppose that Dr. Thomas intended to provide for a museum to gratify public curiosity; but rather to invite contributions of coins, medals, and other articles, that should serve to illustrate American archaeology."

The Civil War brought the museum to another crisis. Clara Barton, the founder of the American Red Cross, presented the Society with a collection of trophies consisting "chiefly of shells and shot of various kinds that have done, or failed to do, their deadly work. Among them is the large torpedo found in Fort Wagner with the hand of a dead soldier attached to the lock, intended to explode when our victorious troops attempt to remove the bodies of the fallen." I have an idea that some gifts of this sort were simply taken out and buried.

After the Civil War, the museum, under the direction of President Salisbury, specialized in art and anthropology. There were numerous gifts of engravings and copies of European works of art. The catalogue of the Society prepared for the World's Fair of 1876 stressed portraits, statues, and busts. In 1880 a sudden interest in American colonial artists and portraits developed. Although this art collection was the only one of its kind in Massachusetts outside of Boston, it was trivial compared with those in the great cities; it contained no original European works of any significance.

On the other hand, the work which the Society was doing in American anthropology in those years was really significant, particularly in the Central American field now that the Smithsonian Institution, the Peabody Museum, and the Bureau of Indian Affairs were primarily attentive to the North American field. It subsidized research, and its meetings were the forum in which the professional anthropologists met and aired the latest ideas. Haven insisted that the chief function of the Society in this field was to publish, but his own principal work was taken over by the Smithsonian. His personal interests were not in the museum, but in the Society's anthropological publications, which were in brisk demand. However, in 1868 a committee expanded the museum into upright glazed cases in the upper hall in which they said they exhibited "nearly all the varieties of Indian utensils and weapons," and there was talk of "completing" the collection of American antiquities, leaving the rest of the world to the Peabody Museum of Cambridge.

Twenty years after the completion of the second building, committees were reporting that it would have to be enlarged, for the museum because of its cramped quarters was becoming distinctly second-class. The space needs of the art museum led to an interesting debate in which it was argued that the requirements of all such collections necessitated architectural bulges which made purely functional buildings necessary. The enlargement provided room for a great collection of Central American photographs, some made systematically by professionals and some snapped eagerly by touring gentlemen with their new cameras. Revolving cases were installed to exhibit the photographs. In 1894 a substantial beginning of a collection of phonograph cylinders of Maya songs was made.

Edward H. Thompson, however, argued that pictures gave but faint ideas of the originals of Maya architecture, and in 1887 he presented the museum with a plaster cast of the doorway façade of the temple at Labna, Yucatan. In the next few years a large collection was made of similar casts of presumably unique "Maya vases, pottery, and obsidian and flint instruments."

After the death of Haven of 1883, the Society officially conceded that its ancient prestige in the field of American archaeology was gone and that the National Museum was doing superbly well the task which had grown too great for a private organization. The use of the museum of the Society by school children, the Council noted, was growing, but its intended use for research had never developed. "Though an historic painter has occasionally sketched an Indian blanket or Hawaiian dress, the collection is practically useless" for historical study. In consequence, perishable materials such as Indian, Icelandic, and Hawaiian apparel were transferred to the Peabody Museum and to the Worcester Society of Antiquity. The exhibition of the Society at the Paris International Exhibition of 1889 did not consist of the "exsiccated Kentucky Indian" and like relics, but a set of its printed *Proceedings,* which won a bronze medal.

The members of the Society who realized how long it had lagged behind the field in American museum progress were anxious to get out of the business, and complained that the segment of the cast of the Labna façade was mistaken for a fireplace by visitors. When the Peabody Museum proposed to erect casts of the entire façade of that temple, the doorway was happily sent to join the other segments. In 1895 the Council stated as its policy "that the museum of the past must be set aside, reconstructed, transformed from a cemetery of bric-a-brac into a nursery of living thoughts."

Such a reconstruction of the museum of the American Antiquarian Society was out of the question, so leading anthropologists and local museum people were called in and invited to take all that their institutions could use. The art museum function of the Society flourished longest, chiefly because some of its leading members never comprehended the problem. After the anthropological material was removed Senator Hoar presented the Society with two fine Greek vases dated by the experts at about 500 B.C. Another gift was a set of life-sized reproductions of Maya frescoes. Moses was renovated at considerable expense in 1900.

The founding of the Worcester Art Museum in 1896, by Salisbury, removed all excuse for the Society's participation in the field of art. When the third building of the American Antiquarian Society was constructed in 1909, no provision was made for a museum. Most of the plaster casts went to the Art Museum, where by 1940 they had disintegrated beyond repair. Moses, after posing for so many years as a historian, was sent to the Worcester County Court House, where, when last I heard, he was still presiding in more appropriate surroundings. In 1928 the last of the uncomfortable historical furniture was turned over to regional institutions. The final distribution of the contents of our museum came in 1964 when local historians of Alabama rediscovered our Alabama Stone, which is perhaps a monument of Spanish exploration, and claimed it as their Plymouth Rock. We happily waived our right to it, and, appropriately enough, they sent a jet plane to pick it up.

So ended the American Antiquarian Society's century and a half in the museum business. Its history is a clear example of the fact that indecision in formulating a collecting policy, failure to adhere to policy, and failure to see one's policy in relation to the policies and resources of others can waste generations of work.

William Clark's
Indian Museum in St. Louis
1816–1838

John C. Ewers

AMERICANS are not accustomed to think of museum men as national heroes. Nevertheless Governor William Clark, founder of the first museum in the trans-Mississippi West, enjoyed that status. No modern astronaut returning from outer space has been more idolized by the American people than were the heroic leaders of the Lewis and Clark Expedition upon their return to St. Louis in 1806, after two years and four months of pioneer overland exploration through the western wilderness and the perilous Indian country to the shores of the Pacific Ocean. In St. Louis, ten years later, Clark established his museum. As its founder and sole proprietor, he was so intimately associated with the museum that one cannot adequately assess the role of the institution without taking into account the career of the man who operated it.

William Clark never made any pretense of scholarship, yet few if any other men of his time possessed a more extensive practical knowledge of the natural history and the Indian tribes of the Great Plains, Rocky Mountains, and Columbia Valley. Born August 1, 1770 on his father's Virginia plantation on the Rappahannock River in Caroline County, Clark received very little formal education, but he quickly became a keen observer of man and nature. He is said to have developed at the age of four a lively interest in Indians which persisted throughout his life. He also learned to draw maps at an early age.[1]

[1] John Bakeless, *Lewis and Clark, Partners in Discovery* (New York, 1947), 9–23.

At 15, William moved westward with his family to Louisville, Kentucky. Four years later he joined his first expedition to fight Indians north of the Ohio, following his famous older brother, George Rogers Clark, eighteen years his senior, into the Army. Commissioned in 1792, William served the next four years as a troop commander and as intelligence officer on detached duty in the wooded wilderness of the Old Northwest and Southwest.[2] In 1796, Lieutenant Clark resigned from the Army and returned home to his Kentucky farm. Here in July 1803 he received a letter from Meriwether Lewis, a former junior officer of his command who had become secretary to President Jefferson. Lewis invited Clark to participate with him in the "fatiegues, dangers, and honors" of leading an official exploring party overland to the Pacific. Clark immediately accepted this challenging offer to join the "Corps of Discovery."[3]

Four years older than Lewis, Clark for all practical purposes enjoyed equal rank with him on the expedition. The introverted, scholarly Lewis was nicely complemented by the outgoing, practical Clark in the joint leadership of this ambitious venture. Lewis had received a quick course of instruction in navigation and biology from Pennsylvania scientists before the Corps of Discovery departed, while Clark served as the expedition's mapmaker—and proved to be a better than average cartographer for his time.[4] Both leaders kept daily journals, and Clark's abominable spelling never kept him from "wrighting." His recently published rough field notes covering the early portion of the outward journey—up the Missouri River to the Mandan villages in present North Dakota, and the winter's sojourn at Fort Mandan in 1804–5—clearly reveal his

[2] *Ibid.*, 28–60.
[3] Donald Jackson, ed., *Letters of the Lewis and Clark Expedition with Related Documents, 1783–1854* (Urbana, Ill., 1962), 57–60, 110–11, 571–72.
[4] Herman R. Friis, "Cartographic and Geographic Activities of the Lewis and Clark Expedition," Washington Academy of Sciences, *Journal*, XLIV (1954), 372–73.

6. Annex of the Second Building of the American Antiquarian Society at Lincoln Square, looking west.

7. General William Clark. Portrait in oil by George Catlin, 1832. Courtesy of Harold McCracken, Cody, Wyoming.

care in observing courses and distances, topographical features, vegetation, and bird, animal, and Indian life. They also tell of his interest in collecting—wild plum seeds for his brother, an antelope "bones and all" for the President, a Yankton Sioux vocabulary.[5]

Specimen collecting was only a minor activity of this first American exploration in the Missouri and Columbia valleys, yet the number and variety of natural history objects and Indian artifacts obtained by Lewis and Clark was noteworthy. About two hundred herbarium specimens are preserved in the Academy of Natural Sciences of Philadelphia, some eighty of which are regarded by botanists as type material. These are either plant specimens collected by Lewis and Clark or plants grown from seeds they brought back.[6] They also forwarded to President Jefferson a number of zoological specimens, including a live prairie dog and two magpies. Some of these were displayed by the President at Monticello; he sent others to Charles Willson Peale for the Philadelphia Museum. A few of the bird and animal specimens are still preserved in the Museum of Comparative Zoology at Harvard, at Vassar College, and at the Academy of Natural Sciences of Philadelphia.[7]

Conspicuous among the articles sent to President Jefferson from the Mandan villages in the spring of 1805 were the oldest known ethnological specimens from the horticultural Mandan, Hidatsa, and Arikara tribes. Several of these anthropological type specimens are exhibited in the Peabody Museum of Archaeology and Ethnology at Harvard.[8] Other Peale Museum ac-

[5] Ernest S. Osgood, ed., *The Field Notes of Captain William Clark, 1803–1805* (New Haven, 1964), 162–63.

[6] Velva E. Rudd, "Botanical Contributions of the Lewis and Clark Expedition," Washington Academy of Sciences, *Journal*, XLIV (1954), 351–56.

[7] Henry W. Setzer, "Zoological Contributions of the Lewis and Clark Expedition," *ibid.*, 356–57.

[8] The list of specimens shipped from the Mandan villages, April 7, 1805, appears in Jackson, ed., *Letters of Lewis and Clark*, 234–36. The ethnological specimens from these collections preserved in the Peabody Museum of Archeology and Ethnology

cessions of Indian artifacts collected by Lewis and Clark, listed in December 1809, include articles from the tribes of the Columbia Valley as well as the plains of the Upper Missouri. From the written descriptions, some of these appear to have been of unusual historic interest, such as "Amulets—taken from the shields of the Blackfoot Indians who attacked Captn. Lewis and were killed by himself and party on the 27th of July 1806 near the Rocky Mountain." Unfortunately, these objects are not known to be preserved.[9]

A careful study of their journals reveals that Lewis and Clark were especially adept at obtaining data on Indian life and customs from native informants. Two modern ethnographers have declared: "They were conscious of their role as social observers, collecting cultural data for scientific purposes. . . . In proper ethnographic style they consistently identified sources of their information and distinguished between data obtained from a member of the subject tribe as compared with that given by neighboring tribesmen. They recognized the Indians as their intellectual equals and they did not ascribe cultural differences to innate characteristics."[10] Clark showed more patience than did Lewis in recording Indian origin myths; no doubt his experience as an intelligence officer aided him in establishing the rapport necessary to obtain detailed, accurate information from the Indians.

President Jefferson soon rewarded the Corps of Discovery leaders with important posts in the new Louisiana Territory, appointing Clark, on March 12, 1807, brigadier general of militia and Lewis to the highest office of Territorial Governor. Lewis, who was to pre-

at Harvard are described in Charles C. Willoughby, "A Few Ethnological Specimens Collected by Lewis and Clark," *American Anthropologist*, New Ser., VII (1905), 633–41.

[9] These specimens are listed in Jackson, ed., *Letters of Lewis and Clark*, 476–79.

[10] Verne F. Ray and Nancy Oestrich Lurie, "The Contributions of Lewis and Clark to Ethnography," Washington Academy of Sciences, *Journal*, XLIV (1954), 358, 360.

pare the official report of the exploration, published a very ambitious prospectus but made little progress on the manuscript before his untimely death in the fall of 1809. Clark, recognizing his own deficiencies as a writer, turned the narrative task over to Nicholas Biddle of Philadelphia. In both correspondence and personal interviews, however, he gave freely of his time to answer the many questions about the expedition and its findings that arose in Biddle's mind as he worked with the journals. Not until 1814 did Biddle's two-volume *History of the Expedition under the Command of Captains Lewis and Clark* appear in print.[11] In 1813 President Madison had appointed General Clark to the office of Governor of the new Missouri Territory. In this position Clark also served as Superintendent of Indian Affairs for the Territory. He occupied this office until Missouri became a state in 1820.

It was during his governorship that William Clark founded his museum in St. Louis. On April 2, 1816, he purchased a lot 120 feet (French measure) in front by approximately 150 feet deep, bounded on the west by Main Street and on the east by the Mississippi Bluffs. Here, at 103 N. Main Street, Clark built a large two-story brick house, one of the finest homes in St. Louis. To the south end of the residence he added a brick wing about 100 feet long and 30 feet wide fronting on 101 N. Main Street. This addition served a double purpose as an Indian council chamber and a museum.[12]

The first description I have found of Clark's Museum must have referred to it very shortly after the new building was completed. It was penned by William C. Preston, a twenty-one-year-old son of a wealthy Virginia family, who visited St. Louis in the course of a 4,000-mile sightseeing tour on horseback through

[11] Jackson, ed., *Letters of Lewis and Clark*, 394–98, 486, 494–555, 562–66, 568–72, 598–600.
[12] Deed Book, "E," Recorder of Deeds, St. Louis, Mo.; J. Thomas Scharf, *History of St. Louis, City and County* (Philadelphia, 1883), 150, 315.

Tennessee, Kentucky, Indiana, Illinois, and Missouri in 1816. General Clark was a friend of the Preston family. He not only entertained young William in his home, but he invited him to witness one of his meetings with picturesque Indian chiefs in his new council chamber.

Preston observed: "On the day of the solemn diplomatic session the Governor's large council chamber was adorned with a profuse and almost gorgeous display of ornamented and painted buffalo robes, numerous strings of wampum, every variety of work of porcupine quills, skins, horns, claws, and bird skins, numerous and large Calumets, arms of all sorts, saddles, bridles, spears, powder horns, plumes, red blankets and flags." Preston also noted: "In the center of the hall was a large long table, at one end of which sat the governor with a sword lying before him, and a large pipe in his hand. He wore the military hat and the regimentals of the army."[13]

Clark must have been eager to display his collections properly, for in July 1818 Henry Rowe Schoolcraft found the museum "arranged with great taste and effect." In addition to collections of Indian "dresses" and "warlike implements," which gave the establishment its common name, Clark's Indian Museum, he also noted such natural history items as "skins of remarkable animals, minerals, fossil-bones, and other rare and interesting specimens."[14] On his return to the museum three years later Schoolcraft observed that "Clark evinces a philosophical taste in the preservation of many objects of natural history, together with specimens of Indian workmanship, and other objects of curiosity collected upon the expedition. . . . We believe that this is the only collection of specimens of art and nature west of Cincinnati, which partakes of the character of a museum, or cabinet of natural history."

[13] Minnie Clare Yarborough, ed., *The Reminiscences of William C. Preston* (Chapel Hill, N.C., 1933), 16.

[14] *A View of the Lead Mines of Missouri* (New York, 1819), 241.

Schoolcraft mentioned "among the specimens which pertain to mineralogy of the country, there are several very fine and large geodes of quartz, lined with crystal and amethyst. These were procured on the river *des Moines* of the Upper Mississippi. Gov. Clark also showed us specimens of granular and foliated gypsum from the Konza."[15]

Clark may have collected a few of the Indian artifacts he first put on display during the Lewis and Clark Expedition, although the great majority of these had been turned over to President Jefferson. Clark soon had an even better opportunity to add to his collection, for in 1821 President Monroe appointed him Superintendent of Indian Affairs at St. Louis, responsible for government relations with all of the northern and western tribes outside the state of Missouri. It was Clark's duty to license Indian traders and to control the issuance of passports to other travelers into the vast Indian regions of the West. In this position, which he held until his death in 1838, the General received not only numerous Indian delegations but many white traders and American and foreign explorers and adventurers who entered the western Indian country through St. Louis, the gateway to the West.

St. Louis, during the period of Clark's Museum, was a small but busy town. It numbered only 5,862 inhabitants in 1830. But it was important both as a Mississippi River port and as an outfitting center for traders, trappers, and explorers of the West. In its streets, shops, and places of entertainment, rough river boatmen mingled with fur traders, mountain men, and Indians—all colorful characters. But to greenhorns from Europe and the East, intent upon exploring the western Indian country on their own, William Clark's Indian Museum, strategically located near the waterfront, was the place where they could obtain an authentic introduction to the Wild West and its resources.

[15] *Travels in the Central Portion of the Mississippi Valley* (New York, 1825), 294.

Their gathering place is listed with typical local pride in Paxton's *St Louis Directory of 1821:* "The Council Chamber of Gov. William Clark, where he gives audiences to the Chiefs of the various tribes of Indians who visit St. Louis, contains probably the most complete Museum of Indian curiosities to be met with anywhere in the United States; and the governor is so polite as to permit its being visited by any person of respectability at any time."

The jovial hero guided many distinguished visitors through his museum, and his enthusiasm, as well as his displays, spurred their interest in the West. In 1823 the German Prince, Herzog Paul Wilhelm von Württemberg, arrived in St. Louis, armed with authority from General Clark's superior, the Secretary of War, to travel in the Indian country of the Upper Missouri. He visited Clark's council chamber,

a room especially arranged for such interviews [with Indians]. This hall is decorated with a great number of Indian weapons, garments, and articles of ornament which Mr. Clark has collected on his journeys from a great number of nations. This collection is very complete and most of its objects, especially the costumes of the tribes of the far west, deserve to be painted and described. Moreover, it is extremely unfortunate that vermin will in a short time destroy the best pieces, especially the beautifully embroidered animal skins.[16]

Prince Paul, himself an artist in pencil, pen-and-ink, and watercolors, subsequently executed the first known drawings of the Upper Missouri. He also collected Indian costumes and other artifacts on this first of his several travels in the American West.[17]

[16] Paul Wilhelm, Prince of Württemberg, "First Journey to North America in the Years 1822 to 1824," trans. William G. Bek, *South Dakota Historical Collections*, XIX (1938), 214–15.
[17] Louis C. Butscher, "A Brief Biography of Prince Paul Wilhelm of Württemberg (1797–1860)," *New Mexico Historical Review*, XVII (1942), 181–225. Prince Paul's original manuscripts and drawings from his travels in the American West, deposited in the Landesbibliothek, Stuttgart, Germany, were destroyed in World War II. His Indian artifacts, preserved in

A more renowned visitor, the Marquis de Lafayette, stopped in St. Louis during his American tour in 1825 and, of course, saw Clark's Museum. His secretary, Auguste Levasseur, was especially impressed by the Indian hunter's necklace of bear claws "from the most terrible of all the animals of the American continent, the Grizzly Bear, of the Missouri" and by an Indian riding whip in which "the knots . . . are very complex, and actually arranged like the knout of the Cossacks." Levasseur wrote, "We could have remained a considerable longer time in Governor Clark's museum, listening to the interesting accounts which he was pleased to give us relative to his great journeys, but we were informed that the hour for dinner had arrived." Nor did the Frenchman fail to record that the American general gave Lafayette "a garment bearing a striking resemblance to a Russian riding coat." It was "made of buffaloe skin, prepared so as to retain all its pliancy."[18]

The most detailed description of Clark's Museum penned by a distinguished visitor was that of Bernhard, Duke of Saxe-Weimar-Eisenach, who saw the collection in 1826:

We then went to see Mrs. Clark, who, through the secretary of her husband, Mr. Alexander, exhibited to us the museum collected by the governor on his travels, and since considerably augmented. Mr. Alexander showed us articles of Indian clothing of different kinds, and various materials,——except the leather, the larger part of these materials were American, or rather entirely European in their origin. A single garment alone, was made by the Cherokees of cotton, which was pulled, spun, wove on a loom, made by an Indian, and even dyed blue by them. Besides, several weapons of different tribes, wooden tomahawks, or battle-axes, in one of them was a sharp piece of iron to strike into the

the Linden Museum in that city, are described and pictured by Walter Krickeberg, "Altere Ethnographica aus Nordamerika im Berliner Museum für Volkerkunde," Baessler Archiv, *Beitrage zur Volkerkunde*, New Ser., II (1954).

[18] *Lafayette in America in 1824 and 1825* (Philadelphia, 1829), II, 124–26.

skulls of their prisoners; another made of elks-horn,
bows of elks-horn and of wood, spears, quivers with
arrows, a spear head of an Indian of the Columbia
river, hewed out of flint, a water-proof basket of the
same people, in which cooking can be performed, several kinds of tobacco pipes, especially the calumet, or
great pipe of peace. The heads of this pipe are cut out of
a sort of argillaceous earth, or serpentine; in time of
war the spot where this earth is dug out, is regarded as
neutral, and hostile parties, who meet each other at
that place, cannot engage in anything inimical against
each other.[19] The pipe which the commissioners of the
United States use at treaties with the Indians, has a
heavy silver head, and a peculiarly handsome ornamented wooden stem. Farther: Mr. Alexander showed
us the medals which the Indian chiefs have received at
different periods from the Spanish, English and American governments, and the portraits of the various
chiefs who have been at St. Louis to conclude treaties
with the governor, who is also Indian agent. Among
the remarkable things in natural history, we noticed an
alligator, eight feet long; a pelican; the horns of a wild
goat, shot by the governor in his tour among the rocky
mountains; the horns of a mountain ram, and those of
an elk, several bearskins, among others, of the white
bear; buffalo, elk, of the skunk, which were sowed together in a robe, skins of martins, ferrets, &c. &c.
moreover, several petrifactions of wood, and animal
subjects, among others, of elephants teeth, a piece of
rock-salt, tolerably white, yet not shooting in crystals,
as the English; various crystals; . . . very handsome
small agates, which are taken for cornelians, &c. Among
the curiosities, the most remarkable were two canoes,
the one of animal-hide, the other of tree bark, a peace
belt, which consists of a white girdle, set with glass
beads two hands breadth wide; farther, snow shoes,
nets which are drawn over an oval frame, also the rack-
ets, which they use in playing their game of ball &c. &c.[20]

Not all travelers who came to St. Louis possessed a
love of museums. Eugène Ney, who reached St. Louis

[19] Following George Catlin's visit to this quarry in 1836, the
red stone the Indians obtained there was named "Catlinite" in
his honor. The site is now part of Pipestone National Monument,
near the town of Pipestone, Minn.
[20] *Travels through North America during the Years 1825 and
1826* (Philadelphia, 1828), II, 101–2.

in June 1830, had become disillusioned with American museums, writing that in the United States

la passion des muséums est générale; chacun veut avoir le sien. Il est vrai de dire qu'on s'y passe cette fantasie à bon marché: un crocodile empaillé suspendu au plafond, un vieil orgue dans un coin, c'est là généralement ce qui constitute leur cabinet de curiosités, avec la pompeuse inscription de MUSEUM en lettres d'or sur la porte.

But he was pleasantly surprised to find that Clark's museum

est très précieuse; elle contient toutes sortes de pelleteries les plus rares, des costumes de sauvages, des armes, des portraits de chefs indiens, des minéraux, des fossiles, etc. Le général en a recueilli lui-même la plus grande partie dans ses voyages; le reste lui a été donné en présent par les diverses tribus indiennes, qui ont toutes pour lui une grande vénération et l'appellent leur père.[21]

It is apparent that this French skeptic's enthusiasm for Clark's Museum was in considerable part a result of his admiration for its heroic proprietor.

Probably no man profited more from his association with General Clark and his museum than did the American artist and amateur ethnologist, George Catlin. Arriving in St. Louis in the spring of 1830 with a letter of introduction to Clark, the thirty-three-year-old Catlin quickly made friends with the sixty-year-old Superintendent of Indian Affairs. In July of that year Catlin accompanied Clark to Prairie du Chien and Fort Crawford, where the general negotiated treaties with the Iowa, Missouri, Sioux, Omaha, and Sauk and Fox tribes. That fall he went with Clark to the Kansa Indians of Kansas River. Doubtless it was Clark, too, who arranged for Catlin to travel to the Pawnee, Omaha, Oto, and Missouri villages on the Missouri and Platte rivers in the spring of 1831. The fol-

[21] "Voyage sur le Mississippi," *Revue des Deux Mondes*, 2d ser., I (1833), 484.

lowing fall Clark offered Catlin an opportunity to meet and to paint portraits of a small delegation of Indians from the vicinity of Fort Union, 2,000 miles up the Missouri, when they passed through St. Louis on their way to visit their Great White Father in Washington. Clark can certainly be credited with introducing Catlin to the Plains Indians.[22] A grateful George Catlin painted William Clark's portrait in 1832. (See plate 7.)

In the early summer of 1832, while en route up the Missouri in the steamboat *Yellowstone*, Catlin painted portraits of two of his fellow passengers, homeward-bound Nez Percé Indians from the Columbia River Valley west of the Rockies. They were returning home from St. Louis, where they had gone to see Clark, the popular "red-head chief" who had visited their people a quarter of a century earlier. Their long trek to St. Louis was of vital significance to the history of the Northwest, for it resulted in the sending of the first missionaries to the Oregon Country, which in turn led to the large-scale emigration of white settlers over the Oregon Trail.[23]

Catlin's observation of the popular interest in Clark's Indian Museum may have encouraged him to augment his hundreds of paintings of Indians with a large collection of artifacts in the Indian Gallery which he exhibited in the larger cities of the East before taking his Gallery to London in 1840 for almost a five year's stand, and on to Paris and Brussels in 1845.[24] Thomas Donaldson, an early student of the life of George Catlin, believed that the Indian artifacts from the Columbia Valley in Catlin's Indian Gallery were formerly a part of Clark's Museum and were given to

[22] John C. Ewers, "George Catlin, Painter of Indians and the West," Smithsonian Institution, *Annual Report for 1955* (Washington, D.C., 1956), 485–86; Loyd Haberly, *Pursuit of the Horizon, A Life of George Catlin, Painter and Recorder of the American Indian* (New York, 1948), 36–47.

[23] Francis Haines, *The Nez Percés, Tribesmen of the Columbia Plateau* (Norman, Okla., 1955), 51–62.

[24] Haberly, *George Catlin*, 101–24, 162–73.

Catlin by William Clark. A few of these specimens are preserved in the United States National Museum.[25] There is nothing in the Museum records, however, to indicate that they were ever actually in Clark's Museum.

Among the newcomers to St. Louis during the winter of 1832–33 was an adventurous Scotsman, Captain (later Sir) William Drummond Stewart of Grand Tully. Stewart was much impressed by Clark's "museum of curiosities, and a collection of arms with the portraits of those who bore them," but his understanding that they were all brought back from the Lewis and Clark Expedition was probably erroneous.[26] Surely no portraitist accompanied the expedition, and it is doubtful that many of the Indian artifacts had actually been collected on the expedition.

For Captain Stewart, St. Louis became the point of departure for a series of almost annual treks westward to the rendezvous of the Rocky Mountain trappers in Wyoming during the decade 1833–43. In 1837 he took along the Baltimore artist, Alfred Jacob Miller, who compiled the only known pictorial record of the life of the picturesque mountain men.[27] The eccentric Stewart surpassed his good friend Clark as a collector of living things. Among his shipments to Scotland were several live buffaloes and several hundred small trees—some from as far away as the Rocky Mountains—for stocking and planting his ancestral estate of Murthly Castle. He also sent Miller to Scotland to execute large oil paintings of scenes in the American West to enliven the walls of the old castle.[28]

[25] Thomas Donaldson, "The George Catlin Indian Gallery in the U.S. National Museum," Smithsonian Institution, *Annual Report for 1855* (Washington, D.C., 1887), 388–89.

[26] "Sir William Drummond Stewart's Description of St. Louis in 1832," *Glimpses of the Past*, I (1934), 31.

[27] Marvin C. Ross, *The West of Alfred Jacob Miller* (Norman, Okla., 1951).

[28] Mae Reed Porter and Odessa Davenport's *Scotsman in Buckskin* (New York, 1963) is a lively biography of Sir William Drummond Stewart.

In March 1833 the able German scientist-explorer, Maximilian, Prince of Wied-Neuwied, described Clark's Indian Museum as it served its other function as a council room for one of Clark's meetings with Indians, in this instance Sauk and Fox tribesmen:

General Clarke invited us to a small assembly, which he was to hold in his house with the Indians. We accordingly repaired thither. This meeting took place in the apartments, which are ornamented with a highly interesting collection of arms and utensils, which the General had procured on his extensive travels with Captain Lewis. The rooms contain, likewise, portraits of the most distinguished Indian chiefs of different nations. General Clarke, with his secretary, was seated opposite to the Indians, who sat in rows along the walls of the apartment. We strangers sat at the General's side, and near him stood the interpreter, a French Canadian. The Indians, about thirty in number, had done their best to ornament and paint themselves; they all looked very serious and solemn, and their chief sat at their right hand. The General first told them, through the interpreter, for what reason he had assembled them here, on which Kiokuck rose, with the calumet in his left hand, gesticulating with his right hand, in harmony with his thoughts; he spoke very loud, in broken sentences, interrupted by short pauses. His speech was immediately translated and written down. This conference lasted above half an hour. General Clarke had introduced us to the Indians, telling them that we had come far over the ocean to see them; they all testified their satisfaction in a rather drawling "Hah," or "Ahah."[29]

Unfortunately, Prince Maximilian's traveling companion, the highly talented Swiss artist, Karl Bodmer, did not sketch this colorful council scene. But the first of his many striking portraits of Indians of the West depicted two participants in this council—The Tortoise, a Sauk; and Eagle's Nest, a Fox Indian.[30] Prince Maximilian and Bodmer went on to ascend the Missouri River as far as Fort McKenzie in the heart of the

[29] *Travels in the Interior of North America in the Years 1832–1834* (London, 1843), 107.

[30] See Plate III of the *Atlas* accompanying Prince Maximilian's text, reproduced here as plate 8.

Blackfoot country, winter among the Mandan, make an extensive collection of Indian artifacts and pencil and watercolor drawings, and gather the material for that exquisitely illustrated classic on the Plains Indians, *Travels in the Interior of North America*, which was published in German, French, and English editions.[31]

On March 13, 1834, the sophisticated New Yorker, Charles Fenno Hoffman, after dining with General Clark, saw the museum with its walls "completely coated with Indian arms and dresses, and the mantlepiece loaded with various objects of curiosity connected with the aborigines. Among the latter was the celebrated piece of pottery that has caused so much idle speculation among the curious—a small vase formed by three perfect heads blended in one, the features being marked, and wholly dissimilar from those of any existing race of Indians."[32]

In addition to descriptions of the collections by prominent visitors there is a fifty-eight-page manuscript catalogue of the collections in the Missouri Historical Society of St. Louis. The first six pages are in William Clark's handwriting, the rest in that of his son, Meriwether Lewis Clark. This catalogue is undated, but the fact that Meriwether Lewis Clark was only seven years of age when the museum was founded in 1816 suggests that it was compiled some years later and perhaps near the end of the museum's twenty-two year history.[33]

---

[31] Prince Maximilian's original field journal and the great majority of Karl Bodmer's magnificent field drawings in pencil and watercolor are in the Joslyn Art Museum, Omaha, Neb. See Marshall B. Davidson, "Karl Bodmer's Unspoiled West," *American Heritage*, XIV (1963), 43–65. Maximilian's Indian artifacts are in the Museum für Volkerkunde, Berlin, and the Linden Museum, Stuttgart. See Krickeberg, "Altere Ethnographica."

[32] *A Winter in the West, by a New Yorker* (New York, 1835), II, 73–74.

[33] Catalogue of Indian Curiosities in William Clark's Museum, Missouri Historical Society, St. Louis. I am indebted to the late Stella M. Drumm, former archivist of that Society, for a typed copy of this document.

William Clark was not above collecting some things which Prince Maximilian would have termed "trifling nicknacks" of more curious interest than scientific significance. Almost every museum of the time had its biological freak, and Clark's was no exception; witness the entry "Double headed Calf's head . . . born at Mr. Wells on the Merimac." But such items are few. This catalogue lists only four geological specimens—one a "Petrified pelt of a tree . . . Obtained in the Osage Country." The number of zoological specimens—other than the animal hides, some of which may have been Indian outer garments—also is quite small. Probably the "feet of a grisly bear . . . Head of Missouri . . . Killed by Govn'r Clark" made a popular conversation piece.

The very great majority of the 201 catalogued items were Indian artifacts, many of which were designated by tribe. The tribes represented included the Cherokee, Chippewa, Choctaw, Delaware, Menomini, Sauk, Shawnee, and Winnebago (woodland peoples, most of whom were removed to the trans-Mississippi West during Clark's Indian Superintendency) ; the Arikara, Assiniboin, Comanche, Hidatsa, Iowa, Mandan, Pawnee, Ponca, Osage, and Oto of the Great Plains; and Taos Pueblo of the Southwest. There was also a "Plaited reed and Sling . . . (the sling made of grass) . . . from Columbia R."

The most common Indian artifacts were pipe stems, of which some forty-five were listed. In Indian ceremonies the stems, not the stone heads, of pipes were the sacred portions. A number of these stems may have been given to the general by Indians, following his councils with them. The most common costume item was moccasins (eighteen pairs), although the catalogue lists no fewer than eleven men's suits (shirts and leggings), as well as two "Squaw's Petticoats," and examples of necklaces, belts, and garters. Ten of the Indian weapons were war clubs (some designated "War Hawk"). There were six bows, three bow covers, three quivers with arrows, three shot pouches, in addition to a spear, a knife, and two scabbards. The largest article of domestic equipment listed was a Sioux lodge presented by the Indian agent, Major Taliaferro, which was painted with a "History of a battle between the Sioux & Pawnees & the Socks Fox." A "Bark Canoe" was also on the list.

Among the considerable number of Indian artifacts entered as presented by Indians, only one was dated —the cotton hunting shirt belonging to Little Terrapin, a Cherokee chief, woven by his wife on a loom the chief made himself and given to Clark at a council in St. Louis, April 29, 1816—the year in which the museum was founded. Many of the Indian artifacts were presented by Clark's white friends—fur traders, Indian agents, and others. A Hidatsa saddle and crupper were given by "M. Charboneau," presumably Toussaint Charbonneau, the interpreter who with his wife Sacajawea accompanied the Lewis and Clark Expedition.

The "portraits of the most distinguished Indian chiefs of different nations" on the walls of the council chamber, which many of the visitors admired, cannot be definitely identified, for the inventory of Clark's estate (1838) carries no record of Indian portraits. Dr. John Francis McDermott, however, thinks it almost certain that Chester Harding's portrait of the Osage chief Sans Nerf, painted in St. Louis in 1820, was originally in Clark's Museum.[34] Perhaps other portraits were by Clark's friend, George Catlin. On their return to St. Louis in 1834, Prince Maximilian and Bodmer examined a collection of Catlin's Indian paintings in the country home of Clark's nephew, Benjamin O'Fallon.[35]

[34] "William Clark: Pioneer Museum Man," Washington Academy of Sciences, *Journal*, XLIV (1954), 372.

[35] Maximilian, *Travels*, 475. Thirty-five Catlin paintings from Major O'Fallon's collection, now in the Chicago Museum of Natural History, have been published in George Quimby, *Indians of the Western Frontier* (Chicago, 1954). They are por-

Some of the Indian rarities described by visitors to Clark's Indian Museum—such as the riding whip which so attracted Lafayette's secretary in 1825, and even the "celebrated piece of pottery" Hoffman mentioned in 1834—also do not appear in the catalogue. One must conclude that it was either an incomplete listing of the items in the collection, or that it listed the collection not long before Clark's death in 1838, after some of the specimens had been given away or otherwise disposed of. The tantalizing fragmentary listing seems to indicate that Clark, the museum man, was a less thorough recorder than had been Clark the field explorer in 1804–6.

In its own time, William Clark's Indian Museum rarely was mentioned apart from its founder and proprietor—the heroic pioneer of American exploration of the West, the beloved "red-head chief" of many western Indian tribes, the highest official of the United States in St. Louis. The museum's active life spanned only twenty-two years, and it did not survive his death. Without Clark's able introduction—and his reputation—the museum's contents would gradually lose their attraction. Perhaps in his last years the exertion of interpreting his collection also began to tell on Clark. At any rate, he or his family apparently began to dispose of the collection before Clark's death.

The *Missouri Saturday News* of February 10, 1838, reports that Meriwether Lewis Clark had deposited "the scientific portion of his father's well known and valuable collection" with the Western Academy of Science in St. Louis. Dr. William Beaumont, noted Army surgeon and a pioneer in research on the role of gastric juices in digestion, rented the museum building and took possession of it on May 1, 1838, exactly four months before William Clark's death.[36]

The fate of the major part of the collection, the

---

traits of Indians Catlin met on his journey up the Missouri in the summer of 1832.

[36] Probate Court, St. Louis, File No. 1416.

8. The Tortoise, a Sauk, and Eagle's Nest, a Fox, members of an Indian delegation who counciled with William Clark in his museum in March 1833. Portraits by Karl Bodmer. From the *Atlas* of Prince Maximilian, *Travels in the Interior of North America in the Years 1832–1834* (London, 1843).

9. The "Infernal Regions" of the Western Museum of Cincinnati. Engraving of 1829. Courtesy of the Cincinnati Historical Society.

10. Hiram Powers, *ca.* 1865. Courtesy of the Cincinnati Historical Society.

Indian artifacts, remains something of a mystery. Dr. McDermott found "no mention of any Indian or other museum objects (save one or two war clubs) in the very detailed papers of William Clark's estate."[37] In the St. Louis *Commercial Bulletin* for December 28, 1837, more than eight months before William Clark's death, it was announced that "Mr. [Albert] Koch, the enterprising proprietor of the St. Louis Museum, has procured many interesting Indian curiosities from the collection of General Clark, and has added them to his valuable establishment." And Koch, who operated his museum in St. Louis from 1836 to 1841, advertised in the same paper on February 22, 1838, his exhibition of "a large collection of Indian curiosities collected by General Clark, which I have received through the liberality and kindness of that gentleman."

The descendants of William Clark, however, passed on a more nefarious interpretation of the matter. In 1911, more than seventy years after General Clark's death, his grandson, William Clark Kennerly, published in his memoirs a brief description of Clark's Indian Museum and the following statement regarding its fate:

It is to be regretted that this collection was not preserved to St. Louis, but about the year 1832 it was borrowed to swell that of a German named Koch, who several years before had arrived in the City with the skeleton of a mastodon and some other curios, opening a museum on Market street near Fourth.

After exhibiting there for a year or more, this "promoter" of his own interests, at least, disappeared between two days with all of the General's collection. It seems strange that no effort was ever made to pursue him and recover them, but, owing to the difficulty of travel, and the fact that Sherlock Holmes' ancestors did not hail from this locality, it was considered hopeless and the said curios now repose in some German museum.[38]

[37] "William Clark," 373.
[38] "Early Days in St. Louis," ed. Mrs. Daniel R. Russell, Missouri Historical Society, *Collections*, III (1911), 408–9.

Similar, but not identical, was the testimony of Clark's great-granddaughter, Miss Eleanor Glasgow Voorhis of New York City (August 11, 1904), based upon a boyhood memory of her eighty-four-year-old great-uncle, James Glasgow, to the effect that

during General Clark's life, this collection was kept intact; afterwards . . . for safe-keeping the collection was sent to a public museum, managed by a man named Koch. After a time, Koch slipped away from St. Louis, taking the collection with him to England, by the way of New Orleans. This fact was not discovered in time to recover the articles; but some years later, one of our family thought that he identified some of them in London.[39]

Not only is Koch's manner of obtaining the "Indian curiosities" not clear, but it is also not known whether he took them with him to Europe when he left St. Louis in 1841, or whether he included them in the portion of his collections sold to William McPherson at that time.[40]

That part of Clark's Indian collection may have been dispersed more widely before or shortly after the general's death is suggested by an entry in the original accession book of John Varden's Washington Museum in the District of Columbia under the date of March 1, 1839, "2 Pipe Stems from the old stock of General Clark of St. Louis, from the Rocky Mountains," which Varden obtained from a Henry W. Flagg on that date in New Orleans. As the Clark Museum catalogue listings reveal, pipestems were the most common artifacts in the collection. In New Orleans, in May 1839, Varden also "received from St. Louis by the S.S. Prairie" a Crow Indian shot pouch, a pair of ornamented garters, a "large Buffalowes skin full of painting," and a "por-

[39] W. Faux, *Journal of a Tour to the United States*, in Reuben Gold Thwaites, ed., *Early Western Travels* (Cleveland, 1905), XI, 263, editor's footnote.

[40] John Francis McDermott, "William Clark's Museum Once More," Missouri Historical Society, *Bulletin*, XVI (1960), 130–33.

trait of an Indian Squaw of the Crow Indians." These may also have come from Clark's Museum.[41]

Another portion of Clark's Indian collection may be preserved in a European collection—not in "Germany" or "London," as the family descendants thought, but in Bern, Switzerland. While examining American Indian collections in Swiss museums in 1907, the American ethnologist, David I. Bushnell, Jr., found and briefly described a choice group of specimens from the tribes of the Upper Missouri, collected by a man named Schoch, who returned from St. Louis to his native city of Bern in 1838 and deposited the materials in the Historical Museum there. Bushnell commented, "According to a note in the museum catalogue all the pieces were obtained directly from Indians. Were it not for this statement it would have been possible to consider some of the material as having come from the old Clark Museum. Such may have been the case, although without definite proof to the contrary we shall probably have to accept the statement in the catalogue as correct."[42]

The *St. Louis Directory* for 1836–37 does list "Schoch, L. A. & Co. dry good store, 4, s. First." The specimens in the Schoch Collection in Bern certainly represent classes of objects—such as Indian shirts, leggings, moccasins, painted robes, and pouches—which were listed in the Clark Museum catalog, but the latter is too fragmentary in its description of specimens to allow of more detailed comparisons. It may never be possible to determine with certainty if the Schoch specimens were ever once a part of Clark's Museum. If they were they must have been some of Clark's finest pieces,

[41] Accession Book of John Varden's Washington Museum, Smithsonian Institution Archives, Washington, D.C. Doubtless all of these specimens, except the portrait of the Crow woman, are preserved in the U.S. National Museum, although complications of cataloguing make it impossible to identify the particular pieces.

[42] "Ethnographical Material from North America in Swiss Collections," *American Anthropologist*, X (1908), 3–5.

for they are of excellent quality and are still well preserved. If they were not, their preservation, along with
the contemporary collections made by George Catlin,
Prince Paul, Prince Maximilian, and other now widely
scattered small Plains Indian collections of the period
of Clark's Museum, renders the disappearance of
Clark's specimens less of a loss to science than would
have been the case had the Clark materials been
unique.

There can be no question of the fate of William
Clark's museum building—the first such structure west
of the Mississippi. It was torn down in 1851 to make
way for the Union Buildings, a "block of six splendid
buildings—designed for warehouses—four stories
high, and fireproof throughout, even to the window
frames, which will be of iron," according to the *Missouri Republican* of January 17. Today the site of William Clark's Indian Museum lies well within the area
of the Jefferson National Expansion Memorial on the
St. Louis waterfront, where the National Park Service,
very appropriately, is developing a museum that will
interpret the history of the trans-Mississippi West.

Interesting as General Clark's collection must have
been to its visitors, it certainly was not the most complete Indian collection in the United States, as the *St.
Louis Directory* of 1821 proclaimed. Charles Willson
Peale's Philadelphia Museum housed 800 American Indian specimens in 1819.[43] And Peale's Museum may
have excelled Clark's even in Plains Indian materials.
Not only did it include the pioneer collections of Lewis
and Clark, transmitted by President Jefferson, but the
Peales continued to add substantial Plains Indian collections during the decade of the 1820's. Thus, in May
1826 Charles Willson Peale purchased from a trader a
"large and complete collection of the Pipes and implements of the Indians of the Missouri and Mississippi."

[43] Charles Coleman Sellers, *Charles Willson Peale*, Vol. II:
Later Life, 1790–1827 (Philadelphia, 1947), 245.

The year after his death in 1827, his sons added more than thirty specimens, mostly articles of costume from the Sioux, Crow, Mandan, Arikara, and Omaha, collected by a Lieutenant Slutter of the United States Army.[44]

Clark's precedent may have influenced the establishment of a similar but smaller museum by the American Fur Company at Fort Union, in the heart of the Indian country, 2,000 miles up the Missouri from St. Louis. The Swiss artist Rudolph Freiderich Kurz, who was employed at Fort Union thirteen years after the demise of Clark's Indian Museum, found that a "number of Indian trinkets are displayed in the reception room and there are, besides, a stuffed Rocky Mountain sheep (female bighorn), black-tailed deer, large white owl, prairie hens, and pheasants, all of which will afford me, meanwhile, sufficient models for sketches and studies."[45] And it was from Fort Union in 1850 that the factor, Edwin T. Denig, and the Culbertson brothers shipped skins, heads, and skulls of typical Upper Missouri mammals to the Smithsonian Institution for its early collections.[46]

Clark's example may have encouraged some of the leaders in the fur trade of the Upper Missouri to make their own collections. We know that James Kipp, an active trader on the Missouri for thirty or more years after 1822, had in retirement on his Missouri farm a fine Indian collection, which was destroyed by fire.[47] Alexander Culbertson, who entered the Upper Missouri trade in 1832 and became the American Fur Company's principal trader in that region, also displayed an Indian collection in his beautiful home, Lo-

[44] Original Accession Book, Peale's Museum, Dec. 4, 1804, to October 1842, Historical Society of Pennsylvania, Philadelphia.

[45] "Journal of Rudolph Friederich Kurz . . . 1846–1852," Bureau of American Ethnology, *Bulletin*, No. 115 (1937), 121.

[46] Edwin Thompson Denig, *Five Indian Tribes of the Upper Missouri*, ed. John C. Ewers (Norman, Okla. 1961), xvii–xviii.

[47] Clyde H. Porter to Frank M. Setzler, Head Curator of Anthropology, U.S. National Museum, Jan. 23, 1950.

cust Grove, near Peoria after his retirement in 1858.[48]

Clark's Museum, nevertheless, was unique in its time in serving a second function as an Indian council chamber. The Indian chiefs and leaders who met Clark there in his official role as Superintendent of Indian Affairs were pleased to find the walls of this meeting place covered with choice articles of Indian art and manufacture and portraits of prominent Indians. These collections must have helped to convince the Indians of Clark's genuine concern for the Indian people and their traditional way of life.

The period of General Clark's Indian Museum was one in which the traditional cultures of the western Indians, enriched by white men's horses and trade goods, flourished, and during which white explorers could establish effective rapport with the Indians. It was the Golden Age of western exploration by energetic and able men on their own initiative, before the wholesale invasion of the Indian hunting grounds by white emigrants and settlers resulted in broken treaties and bloody Indian wars. William Clark and his museum, standing at the gateway to the West, helped to make that Golden Age.

[48] Anne McDonnell, ed., "The Fort Benton Journal, 1854–1856," Historical Society of Montana, *Contributions*, X (1940), 241–42.

"Ohio Show-Shop"
The Western Museum of Cincinnati
1820–1867

Louis Leonard Tucker

THE Western Museum of Cincinnati was founded in 1820 and expired in 1867.[1] The first of its type to be established in the trans-Allegheny country, the Western Museum passed through the same historical transitions as Peale's, Scudders', and other noted museums in the East. For the first three years of its existence it operated exclusively as a center of science; administered by scientifically oriented men, the Museum was committed to the ideal of extending man's knowledge of the natural world. During this period it attracted few patrons and seemed destined for early dissolution. For the remaining forty-four years of its existence it maintained a scientific façade but actually functioned on the premise that a museum should entertain, enthrall, and frighten patrons, not enlighten or educate them. It became, in short, a typical American museum. As a perceptive English visitor put it:

[1] This article is based upon materials housed in the Cincinnati Historical Society, Cincinnati, Ohio, hereafter cited as CHS. Brief accounts of the Western Museum can be found in most of the standard works on the history of Cincinnati, but none is satisfactory. They are studded with factual errors and lack genetic development. A carefully researched, but limited, disjointed, and amateurish article is that of Elizabeth Kellogg, "Joseph Dorfeuille and the Western Museum," Cincinnati Society of Natural History, *Journal*, XXII (1945). A sketchy survey of the "scientific era" of the Western Museum can be seen in Walter B. Hendrickson, "The Western Museum Society," Historical and Philosophical Society of Ohio (now CHS), *Bulletin*, VII (1949), 99–110. Of less value is Bruno Gebhard, "From Cincinnati's Western Museum to Cleveland's Health Museum," CHS, a reprint from *Ohio State Archaeological and Historical Quarterly*, LIX (1950), 371–84.

A "Museum" in the American sense of the word means a place of amusement, wherein there shall be a theatre, some wax figures, a giant and a dwarf or two, a jumble of pictures, and a few live snakes. In order that there may be some excuse for the use of the word, there is in most instances a collection of stuffed birds, a few preserved animals, and a stock of oddly assorted and very dubitable curiosities; but the mainstay of the "Museum" is the "live art," that is, the theatrical performance, the precocious mannikins, or the intellectual dogs and monkeys.[2]

Vulgarized and converted into a freak and horror show, the Western Museum became one of the best-known entertainment sites in the United States and the first Disneyland of the West.

The founding of the Museum was closely linked to the phenomenal economic boom Cincinnati experienced following the appearance of the steamboat on the Ohio River in 1811.[3] By 1820 Cincinnati was the steamboat capital of the Ohio Valley and on its way to becoming the economic colossus of the Middle West. Here was the quintessence of "Boomtown, U.S.A." Those areas of America's heartland which were tied to the inland river transportation network would soon feel the effects of Cincinnati's booming, diversified economy. Cairo would keep itself clean with Cincinnati soap. Hannibal would live in Cincinnati prefabricated houses. Memphis would subscribe to Cincinnati newspapers. Vicksburg would drink Cincinnati whiskey. New Orleans would eat Cincinnati pork. Everybody in the West would read Cincinnati McGuffey *Readers*. In 1820 the pattern was being laid for future greatness. The population had expanded to 9,642 residents, and

[2] Edward Hingston, *The Genial Showman, Being Reminiscences of the Life of Artemus Ward* (London, 1870), I, 11–12.

[3] The bibliography on the early history of Cincinnati is extensive. The most accurate, but not the most stylistically graceful, secondary account is Charles T. Greve, *Centennial History of Cincinnati and Representative Citizens* (Chicago, 1904). For a racy, journalistic-type history, see Alvin F. Harlow, *The Serene Cincinnatians* (New York, 1950); it is strong in interpretation but weak in factual accuracy.

the city contained five printing offices, four book and stationery stores, ten churches—and seventeen taverns!

But life in Cincinnati was not all work and drink. The "Tyre of the West" was already showing demonstrable signs of its eventual metamorphosis into the "Athens of the West," a status it would achieve in the 1840–60 period. Few other American cities, East or West, experienced a similar cultural flowering in so short a span of time. A myriad of cultural, scientific, and intellectual agencies sprang into existence as material prosperity increased and men of wealth appeared. With the blunting of the crudities of frontier life, the elite of Cincinnati turned to "things of the mind," to cultural and scientific diversions. Out of this development grew the Western Museum.

Like all institutions, museums reflect the values of those who establish and administer them. Before the Western Museum passed into its "hokum" phase, it mirrored the aspirations and ideals of Daniel Drake, one of its prime founders.[4] Drake was a doctor by profession, but he was something more than a mender of bones. Known to his contemporaries as the "Benjamin Franklin of the West," he aspired to make Cincinnati the cultural and intellectual capital of the trans-Allegheny country. Philadelphia, where he had studied medicine, served as his model for emulation. Pugnacious in personality, progressive in intellectual outlook, Drake either founded, or inspired the formation of, every major cultural, scientific, and educational institution in Cincinnati in the 1820–40 period. Through his research and writings, he also established himself as one of the most eminent scientists of the West. He was

[4] On Drake, see Emmet F. Horine, *Daniel Drake (1785–1852), Pioneer Physician of the Midwest* (Philadelphia, 1961); Samuel D. Gross, *A Discourse on the Life, Character and Services of Daniel Drake, M.D.* (Louisville, Ky., 1853); Otto Juettner, *Daniel Drake and His Followers, Historical and Biographical Sketches* (Cincinnati, 1909); Edward D. Mansfield, *Memoirs of the Life and Services of Daniel Drake, M.D.* (Cincinnati, 1855).

one of the few westerners holding membership in the American Philosophical and Geological societies and in the Philadelphia Academy of Natural Sciences. He also served as a counselor of the prestigious American Antiquarian Society of Worcester, Massachusetts.

A man who grasped life by the throat, and some of his detractors as well, Drake was a prototypal liberal of the American Enlightenment. A volatile, versatile dynamo, he dared to challenge the status quo in all areas of community life, and as a result his career was a chronicle of controversy. While not totally successful in his efforts to transform a materialistically inclined river town into an "Athens of the West," Drake achieved some remarkable successes.

Other Cincinnatians, notably William Steele, first expressed the belief that the city needed a scientific museum, but it was Drake who transformed idea into action. Prodded on by the scientist-doctor, in 1818 a group of learned Cincinnatians began assembling a collection of shells, fossils, foreign coins, Indian artifacts, Egyptian oddities, and the like. Drake contributed his own extensive cabinet of fossils, shells, and Indian articles. All of these items were neatly arranged in exhibition cases in rooms rented in the building occupied by Cincinnati College, now known as the University of Cincinnati.

On June 10, 1820, the Museum was formally dedicated. Drake delivered the main address.[5] His speech did not embody conventional hortatory pap. Rather, it was an articulate presentation which outlined the objectives of the new society and the programs to be developed. In a larger sense, it was one of the seminal scientific pronouncements in the American West in the early nineteenth century.

Drake's ambitious plan called for the collection and

[5] *Anniversary Discourse on the State and Prospects of the Western Museum Society* (Cincinnati, 1820); Drake dedicated the pamphlet to Steele and acknowledged him to be the inspiring agent and the most generous contributor.

preservation of "natural and artificial curiosities" embracing "nearly the whole of those parts of the great circle of knowledge" and appealing to the "naturalist, the antiquary and the mechanician." These items would be obtained from all sections of the United States with a special emphasis on the Ohio Valley. The collection was to be carefully arranged in conformity with the scheme of classification developed by the noted scientist, Joseph Lancaster. Drake reported that artifacts already procured had been classified on the basis of the Lancastrian system.

Collecting and arranging were but peripheral activities in the program of the Museum. Drake affirmed that the Museum had more profound responsibilities than merely to become "a complete school for natural history." It should activate programs in all major areas of scientific investigation, particularly archaeology, natural history, zoology (stress on ornithology), mineralogy, and geology.

Drake fleshed out his generalizations with specific projects. In paleontology, for example, he urged that the Museum conduct investigations at nearby Big Bone Lick, Kentucky, and develop a collection of the bone specimens of the prehistoric monsters which were buried at that important site, and that these specimens should be augmented by others acquired from all parts of the United States. The ultimate goal would be to assemble the most complete collection of skeletal remains of the massive prehistoric animals which once existed in the United States. In Drake's judgment, Cincinnati was the most logical site in the "Western Country" for housing such a collection.

A torrent of ideas and programs cascaded from Drake's vibrant mind. The mineralogy and geology of Ohio and the Valley should be analyzed. The ancient Indian cultures of the Ohio Valley, notably that of the Mound Builders, should be studied. The Museum should promote fine arts "in a manner that will both delight and refine the public taste." It should also encourage "useful and ornamental arts" by collecting and displaying drawings, models, and products. A collection of scientific instruments should be acquired to illustrate the principles of magnetism, electricity, galvanism, hydrostatics, optics, and the mechanics of the solar system. A lecture series on natural history should be conducted. A library of scientific works should be developed. In Drake's words: "Thousands of years have elapsed since the students of Nature began to unfold her mysteries. Books are the great repository of their discoveries, and he who neglects them, begins, like the first observer, unaided and alone."

The relationship of the Museum to Cincinnati College, Drake observed, represented a natural union and should be strengthened: "The College is principally a school of literature, the Museum of science, and the arts. The knowledge imparted by one is elementary, by the other practical. Without the former, our sons would be illiterate; without the latter, they would be scholars merely—by the help of both, they may become scholars and philosophers." Further indication of his plan to develop strong ties between the Museum and the College was an agreement Drake had drawn up with the College trustees on March 28, 1819, which provided for the free use of the facilities of the Museum and holdings by students and professors.[6] Drake's eventual objective was clear-cut: He aspired to make the Museum—and Cincinnati—the scientific capital of the West.

Drake terminated his address with a passionate appeal for America to declare its intellectual independence from Europe. Further reflecting the nascent nationalism of his generation, he affirmed the future greatness of the United States, but cautioned that such greatness was contingent upon scientific progress:

[6] The terms of the agreement are printed in William H. Venable, *Beginnings of Literary Culture in the Ohio Valley, Historical and Biographical Sketches* (Cincinnati, 1891), 310–11.

"Let the architects of our national greatness conform to the dictates of science; and the monuments they construct will rise beautiful as our hills, imperishable as our mountains, and lofty as their summits, which tower sublimely above the clouds."

And so the Museum opened its doors under the active direction of two young curators. The chief curator was a young English scientist, Dr. Robert Best, who also held a position on the staff of Cincinnati College.[7] The second in command was John James Audubon, newly arrived from Kentucky at the urging of Drake.[8] Audubon's main responsibility was the mounting of birds and fishes. When not functioning as a taxidermist he wandered through the verdant countryside, sketching animals and birds—laying the groundwork for one of the most spectacular careers in ornithology in world history. Drake and four other prominent Cincinnatians functioned as "Managers" and established general policy. The basic organization of the Museum was that of a stock company, each member owning shares to the value of $50. Members and their families were permitted to enter the Museum free of charge. Adult visitors were assessed an entry fee of 25 cents; children were admitted at half price.

During the first years of operation the scientific orientation of the Museum remained as firmly fixed as the North Star. Drake's influence was dominant. At the second anniversary of the Western Museum Society on June 10, 1822, a poetic offering titled "An Ode to Science" was delivered. Overflowing with sentiments of

[7] Best later had a brief but distinguished career as a professor of chemistry at Transylvania University in Lexington, Kentucky. He became a "nervous wreck" and died in 1830 at the age of forty.

[8] On Audubon's brief period in Cincinnati, see Alice Ford, *John James Audubon* (Norman, Okla., 1964), 111–13; Stanley C. Arthur, *Audubon, An Intimate Life of the American Woodsman* (New Orleans, 1937), 96–99. Arthur states that it was during his Cincinnati residence that Audubon was seized by the "Great Idea" to draw from nature a "comprehensive and complete collection of all the birds of the United States."

provincial pride and expressing the typical ebullient optimism of the Enlightenment, the poem constituted a grandiloquently phrased reaffirmation of Drake's address of 1820. The concluding two stanzas suggest the character of the "Ode to Science" :

Great Genius of Science! we ask thy direction
   In guiding our footsteps in every pursuit:
Man is raised to an *angel* beneath thy protection,
   And, without it, is sunk to a *savage* or *brute.*

And whilst we acknowledge, with heartfelt emotion,
   That praise to thy throne should for ever rise,
Press this truth on our minds, in the midst of devotion—
   The pathway of Science conducts to the Skies.[9]

At the outset, Cincinnatians and river travelers willingly paid 25 cents for admission to gape at what was one of the largest and best-arranged scientific collections in America—a collection then valued at $4,000. Additional specimens of "natural and artificial curiosities" were procured from other sections of the United States and foreign lands. In October 1822, for example, the Museum acquired "between 3 and 400 Birds and Quadrupeds, (principally foreign,) a large number of Reptiles, Shells, Coins, Medals, Egyptian and Roman Adtiquities [*sic*], among others, the head of an Egyptian Mummy, found in the catacombs of the celebrated Thebes in Upper Egypt, a number of Egyptian Manuscripts on Sapyrus [*sic*], Vases, household Gods, Dei Lares, ancient Coins of Roman Emperors."[10] By 1823 the collection was highlighted by 100 mammoth and Arctic elephant bones; 50 *Megalonyx* bones; 33 quadrupeds; 500 birds; 200 fishes; 5,000 invertebrates; 1,000 fossils; 3,500 minerals; 325 botanical specimens; 3,125 medals, coins, and tokens; 150 Egyptian and 215 Indian artifacts; 112 microscopic designs; views of American scenery; about 500 specimens of fine arts; 1 elegant organ; and 1 head of a South Sea island chief

[9] Published pamphlet, anonymous, CHS.
[10] *Cincinnati Inquisitor and Advertiser*, Oct. 8, 1822.

"preserved and beautifully tatooed by the Cannibals of New Zealand."[11] The collection of scientific works in the library was also expanded with the help of Yale's Benjamin Silliman and other noted academic scientists in the East. There was as much truth as provincial pride in the boastful statement of one Cincinnati newspaper that the Museum had a "greater variety of specimens, a neater and more classical arrangement of curiosities than any institution of its kind and age in the United States."[12]

By 1823, however, Drake's vision of the Museum as a center of western science crashed headlong into the unyielding reality of operating expenses. Creditors preferred hard cash to eloquent words. An economic depression, public apathy toward nondramatic scientific exhibits, and the diversion of Drake's interest by a host of personal problems and public controversies led to the near demise of the Museum. The managers agreed to sell the collections,[13] but were surprised to discover that there were no buyers. Ultimately they decided to give the collection to a newly employed curator, Joseph Dorfeuille, on the condition that they and the stockholders and their families be admitted to the Museum free of charge. Dorfeuille agreed to the condition, assumed ownership, and promptly moved the Museum to a site close to the public landing, the most vibrant area of the city. With the change of ownership and location, the Western Museum entered the second and final phase of its history—the age of hokum.[14]

Joseph Dorfeuille was one of those learned, peripatetic Frenchmen who flit across the pages of nineteenth-century western history with marked frequency.[15] His background is shrouded in mystery. Some

[11] Museum handbill, CHS.

[12] *Liberty Hall and Cincinnati Gazette*, Sept. 30, 1823.

[13] *Ibid.*, March 18, 1823.

[14] To stimulate attendance, Dorfeuille reduced the annual subscription price. See *ibid.*, Aug. 5, 1823.

[15] The most extensive account of Dorfeuille is that in Kellogg, "Dorfeuille and Western Museum."

said that he was born in France of noble birth, a nephew of the Duchesse de Richelieu, no less. Others said that he was native-born, and a charlatan to boot. There were other theories circulating on Dorfeuille's background—that he had been involved in the ill-fated French settlement at Gallipolis, Ohio; that he was from New Orleans; that he was from Pennsylvania; that he was a Swabian named Dorfel who had changed his name when he learned how enthusiastic Cincinnatians were about Frenchmen. Whatever the truth about Dorfeuille's birthplace and background, everyone agreed that his was a captivating personality. Even Madame Frances Trollope, the acerbic English critic of Cincinnati's "domestic manners" and residents, conceded that Dorfeuille was "a man of taste and science."[16] Scientist, musician, artist, lecturer—Dorfeuille was a coruscant, multifaceted "character"—sophisticated, cultured, catholic in his interests. In the words of William Henry Venable, he was "a cyclopedia of popular knowledge who gave didactic addresses on language, books, birds and I know not what besides."[17] Contemporary Cincinnati newspapers and literary and scientific journals lauded his scholarship and wide scope of knowledge. His main scientific foci were paleontology, conchology, entomology, and teratology.[18] He was a regular contributor to local scientific journals and took an active part in local scientific activities. The full range of his scientific interest is revealed by a scrapbook he compiled; the document is now the property of the Cincinnati Historical Society. The scrapbook contains many high-quality engravings relating to a multitude of scientific subjects, from the Mound Builders of the Ohio Valley to the most grotesque teratological representations recorded in history.

[16] *Domestic Manners of the Americans,* ed. Donald Smalley (New York, 1949), 62.

[17] *Literary Culture in Ohio Valley,* 68.

[18] *Western Quarterly Reporter of Medical Surgical and Natural Science,* I (1822), 312, 398–400.

Along with the compilation of a scientific scrapbook, Dorfeuille accumulated an extensive collection of natural history specimens. These activities long preceded his arrival in Cincinnati, for he had supported himself by exhibiting these items as he traveled. Assuming control of the Western Museum, he reorganized its collection and incorporated his own holdings, making it the fourth largest museum in the country. A poetic effort of less than brilliant quality provides us with an insight into the revitalized Western Museum under the curatorship of Monsieur Dorfeuille:

Wend hither, ye members of polished society—
    Ye who the bright phantoms of pleasure pursue—
To see of strange objects the endless variety,
    Monsieur Dorfeuille will expose to your view.
For this fine collection, which courts your inspection,
    Was brought to perfection by his skill and lore,
When those who projected and should have protected
    Its interests, neglected to care for it more.

Here are pictures, I doubt not, as old as Methusalem,
    But done in what place I can't say, nor by whom;
Some of which represent certain saints of Jerusalem,
    And others, again, monks of Venice and Rome;
Old Black Letter pages of far-distant ages,
    Which puzzled the sages to read and translate,
And manuscripts musty, coins clumsy and rusty,
    Of which time, untrusty, has not kept the date.

Lo, here is a cabinet of great curiosities,
    Procured from the Redmen, who once were our foes;
Unperished tokens of dire animosities,
    Darts, tomahawks, war-cudgels, arrows and bows,
And bone-hooks for fishes and old earthen dishes,
    To please him who wishes o'er such things to pore,
Superb wampum sashes, and mica-slate glasses,
    Which doubtless the lasses much valued of Yore.[19]

While intellectually committed to science, Dorfeuille was also of a practical bent. He realized that museums of his day did not live by science alone, that fossils, shells, and Indian relics might lure a patron once but

[19] *Cincinnati Literary Gazette*, I (March 13, 1824), 88.

no more. For the general public, especially the "country customers," the "truths of natural science were not as attractive . . . as the occasional errors of nature in her productions."[20] The masses craved novelty and a touch of the bizarre, and "Old Oyster Shell," as Dorfeuille's employees referred to him, was prepared to cater to their wishes, Then, too, Dorfeuille was faced with the problem of competition. There was a second museum in Cincinnati, Letton's, and it specialized in the unique and sensational type of exhibit.[21] Its star attraction was an ancient Negro woman who, in 1835, claimed to be 161 years of age and an ex-slave of George Washington's father!

Dorfeuille did not completely abandon the cause of science during his period of ownership. For example, he presented public lectures on a variety of scientific subjects. One of his presentations, "The Pleasures Arising from the Study of Natural History and the Fine Arts," was so well received (especially by the ladies) that he was frequently requested to repeat it. He also brought in capable academicians from Transylvania University of Lexington, Kentucky, formerly the scientific center of the West, to lecture on traditional scientific subjects. On occasion their lectures wandered into the realm of popular science—phrenology, for example.

But serious science was no longer the main business of the Museum. Dorfeuille set it off on a commercial tack and it kept a steady course. Education became incidental. The scientific collections were maintained, even expanded, but they were no longer the featured attraction. Innovation and novelty characterized the new era, and it took many forms. One of the first additions made by Dorfeuille was the always popular waxworks exhibit. As Mrs. Trollope observed, Cincinnatians "have a most extravagant passion for wax

[20] *Genius of the West, An Original Magazine of Western Literature,* IV (1855), 195.

[21] On Letton's Museum, see Greve, *Centennial History,* I, 538.

figures."[22] Some thirty figures of "this barbarous branch of art" were acquired and scattered among the cases of geological and entomological specimens. National political leaders were juxtaposed with Indian chiefs and monsters. In one corner stood a set of figures depicting the Cowan family of Cincinnati. Mr. Cowan had achieved a measure of local notoriety by embedding a hatchet in the skulls of his wife and two children. The dramaturgical scene portrayed Cowan in the act of doing his wife in, while the slain children weltered in a bloody pool. A note of authenticity made the grisly exhibit even more spectacular: Mr. Cowan wielded the actual murder weapon, while Mrs. Cowan was adorned in the bonnet and dress worn on that fateful day. "Old Oyster Shell" had gone to great lengths to secure these items.[23]

For those whose appetites for the macabre were still not sated, Dorfeuille established a special Chamber of Horrors which contained, among other appetizing attractions, the head, right hand, and heart of Mathias Hoover, a murderer of local renown. These items were immersed in alcohol in three "appropriate vases." Dorfeuille was quick to assure his patrons that the presence of Hoover's remains in the Museum was not an effort on his part to capitalize on sensationalism. As he explained in a newspaper advertisement:

It may, perhaps, be already known that *Mathias Hoover*, the Murderer, previous to his execution, bequeathed his body to the proprietor of the Western Museum for the express purpose of its being exhibited publicly, as a warning to others of the awful risk, attending a departure from the paths of virtue. Such being the case, his wish has been complied with as far

[22] *Domestic Manners*, ed. Smalley, 62.
[23] Linden Ryder to Hiram Powers, Nov. 21, 1835, Powers Papers, Box 4, CHS. Cowan's crime was one of the most sensational of the period. On the day he was hanged, he acknowledged his guilt to a crowd estimated between 20,000 to 30,000 people. He blamed his action on "intemperance" and warned all to "beware of the seducing bowl." See *Buckeye and Cincinnati Mirror*, V (Nov. 28, 1835), 39.

as possible and such parts of his body have been preserved and prepared for public inspection as could be effected consistently with a sense of what is due to the feelings of the visitors of that establishment.[24]

A concluding statement, that admission to the Museum was 25 cents "without distinction of age," may have been seemingly tactless juxtaposition, but it did emphasize a point already well known to Cincinnatians: Dorfeuille placed as much value on a profit and loss sheet as he did on promoting public virtue.

The waxworks exhibit was not exclusively confined to grisly murder scenes. For those timid souls who preferred violence without bloodshed, and a bit of history to boot, Dorfeuille presented Aaron Burr in the process of dispatching his arch rival, Alexander Hamilton. For historically minded purists he offered John Quincy Adams, George Washington on his death bed, and General Andrew Jackson being crowned by the "Beauty of Cincinnati." Devotees of romantic literature could gaze upon a pensive Prince on tiptoe meditating his kiss over a reclining Sleeping Beauty. There was something for everybody.[25]

The exhibit of wax figures became one of the most popular features of the Museum. Its success was at least partially due to Hiram Powers, the "sublime mechanic," who joined Dorfeuille's staff in 1829.[26] Born and raised in Vermont, Powers accompanied his family to Cincinnati in 1819. Here, at the age of fourteen, he began the "battle of life" in a produce store where he demonstrated a creative urge (and impish sense of

[24] *Liberty Hall and Cincinnati Gazette,* July 4, 1837.

[25] Contemporary newspapers and Museum handbills list the chief wax figures. See also William Henry Venable, "Going Down to Cincinnati," *The Hesperian Tree,* ed. John J. Piatt (Cincinnati, 1900), 136–37.

[26] The major source for Powers' life and career is the collection of Powers Papers (four boxes) in the CHS. It includes over seven hundred manuscript letters, contemporary newspaper clippings from all parts of the United States, and other printed matter. As yet, Powers has not received extensive biographical treatment.

humor) by opening firkins of butter and modeling the ductile esculent into such horrid forms as "gasping loggerheads" and "hissing" rattlesnakes; he then replaced the covers. His next employment with a clock and organ manufacturer provided him with a springboard for future fame, as his native mechanical aptitude flowered during this phase of his career. The clocks he constructed are now prized as collectors' items.

While working as a clockmaker, Powers chanced to visit Dorfeuille's Museum, where he became intrigued by a plaster cast of Houdon's Washington, the most popular piece of statuary in America at the time. Stimulated by this experience, he decided to learn the art of making plaster casts and placed himself under the tutelage of a competent German artist in Cincinnati. Power's practical bent soon merged with the artistic, and he began producing casts of a higher quality than those of his instructor.

Dorfeuille, among the first to detect the creative potential of the youngster, induced him to work part-time in the Museum as a restorer of waxworks. Dorfeuille had been procuring his wax models from New Orleans. After being tossed about on the long steamboat journey, the figures were usually in a "very promiscuous condition" when they reached Cincinnati. So skillful was Powers in restoring the wax models that Dorfeuille was soon wooing him as a full-time employee. In 1829 the twenty-four-year-old Powers left the employ of the clockmaker and joined Dorfeuille's staff as "inventor, wax-figure maker, and general mechanical contriver." Powers became the answer to Dorfeuille's prayers. He not only repaired wax figures, he also created them—and with such precision that they often could not be distinguished from human beings. One of his best likenesses was a figure of Dorfeuille himself.

Power's extraordinary abilities as both artist and technician were significant factors in the early success of the Museum, but they were complemented by Dorfeuille's acumen as a promoter. One illustration is in order. While serving as a part-time employee, Powers was directed to repair some wax figures which had been damaged in shipment. The figures were so battered as to be unrecognizable, and Powers and Dorfeuille decided that new figures should be made from them. Powers proposed to take the head of Lorenzo Dow and convert it into the "King of the Cannibal Islands." Dorfeuille was to take the body and "fit body to fit head." Powers related the conclusion of this episode as follows:

I took the head home, and, thrusting my hand into the hollow, bulged out the lanky cheeks, put two alligator's tusks into the place of the eyeteeth, and soon finished my part of the work. A day or two after, I was horrified to see large placards upon the city-walls, announcing the arrival of a great curiosity, the actual embalmed body of a South-Sea man-eater, secured at immense expense, etc. I told my employer that his audience would certainly tear down his museum, when they came to find out how badly they were sold, and I resolved myself not to go near the place. But a few nights showed the public to be very easily pleased. The figure drew immensely, and I was soon, with my old employer's full consent, installed as inventor, wax-figure maker, and general mechanical contriver in the museum.[27]

Dorfeuille also displayed his acumen as a promoter with respect to new acquisitions, which adhered to one criterion: they must excite the emotions, not titillate the intellect. In striving to build a "bigger and better" museum he added a "real Mermaid which was first procured at Bencoolen, and afterwards exhibited in England at a Guinea a head; and from thence in every state of our Union, to the eager curiosity of thousands who flocked to see and judge for themselves of this wonder of the deep"[28]—(stuffed, of course, but the gul-

[27] Henry W. Bellows, "Seven Sittings with Powers, the Sculptor," *Appleton's Journal of Popular Literature, Science and Art* (June 12–Sept. 11, 1869), Sitting 3, in Powers Papers, Box 4.
[28] Museum handbill, CHS.

lible hog drovers who flocked into "Porkopolis" never suspected it) ; the very cudgel with which Captain Cook had been killed; some rusty keys taken from a robbers' cave in southern Illinois; and dazzling pictures of Circassian girls, seen through magnifying glasses fixed in the wall. And, of course, he added conventional monstrosities—a pig with eight feet, seven legs, and two tails, two-headed snakes, geese, and chickens, and others. Even Barnum would have been envious of such acquisitions.

There were still other innovations. Dorfeuille introduced the practice of concluding his lectures on natural history by having his audience sniff nitrous oxide, or laughing gas.[29] Always seeking new and more spectacular forms of entertainment, Dorfeuille once hired a ventriloquist; after one week's performances he was throwing his voice around an empty room, and he was out of a job.[30] Of even briefer duration was the engagement of an itinerant Polish artist who balanced a thick stick on his chin while holding cannon balls on his finger tips.[31] To celebrate the Fourth of July, the enterprising Dorfeuille hired local military bands, and the Museum vibrated to the pulsating sounds of patriotic songs.

The "Invisible Girl," developed in 1828, was one of Dorfeuille's more successful promotions.[32] Combining "literary allusion, Oriental hocus pocus and Georgian beau-monde charade," this dramatic entertainment was the brain child of Mrs. Trollope. Initially, children

[29] *Liberty Hall and Cincinnati Gazette*, Jan. 24, 1823.

[30] Ryder to Powers, March 3, 1837, Powers Papers, Box 4. The ventriloquist worked with a partner who told stories. He, too, failed to "startle the mobility" and was discharged.

[31] Ryder to Powers, May 22, 1836, *ibid.*, Box 2.

[32] *Cincinnati Gazette*, April 8, 12, 18, 1828. Mrs. Trollope's involvement in this enterprise is discussed in Trollope, *Domestic Manners*, ed. Smalley, xxvii–xxviii. Not to be outdone, a rival museum staged an exhibit titled "The Haunted Castle or Invisible Lady." This mysterious lady also answered questions in foreign languages, and additionally, "she will blow out a candle and whisper." *Cincinnati Gazette*, April 18, 1828.

were not permitted to witness the exhibit; subsequently, Dorfeuille relented and allowed them to observe the spectacle—at adult prices! Season subscribers also had to pay a special admittance fee. Twelve patrons at a time were led into a darkened room which was furnished in the fashion of an ancient Egyptian theater. Each patron was permitted to address three questions to the invisible oracle, "Pythia," who responded in one of seven foreign languages, her voice appearing to emanate from all parts of the room. The "philosophical experiment," as Dorfeuille described the show, lasted for eight weeks and attracted many customers. The identity of the oracle became the mystery of the day in Cincinnati. It was finally discovered that the "Invisible Girl" was really Mrs. Trollope's precocious son Henry, who up to that time had found his multilingual abilities to be of no value in Porkopolis. Only on one other occasion did Henry make a "cultural" impact on Cincinnati. He gave an unforgettable performance as Sir John Falstaff in Shakespeare's *Merry Wives of Windsor*—unforgettable because he was "very drunk" at the time.

The "Invisible Girl" was followed by another "stupendous and colossal" entertainment. Designated by such titles as "Dorfeuille's Hell," "Dante's Inferno," "the Infernal Regions," and, most commonly, "the Regions," it became the most celebrated single attraction staged by an American museum in the pre-Civil War era.[33] A number of people were involved in the enterprise. While direct evidence is lacking, there is a strong suspicion that Mrs. Trollope supplied the central concept for the exhibit.[34] Her protégé and traveling com-

[33] The best sources for "the Regions" are contemporary newspapers, Museum handbills, and Hiram Powers correspondence, all in CHS.

[34] Donald Smalley is convinced of this and the evidence seems to bear him out. Smalley calls Mrs. Trollope the "anonymous dictator" of Cincinnati amusement. See Trollope, *Domestic Manners*, ed. Smalley, xxviii–xxxiv; there is an excellent contemporary description of "the Regions" by a Boston visitor on pp. 63–64, note.

panion in America, a young French artist by the name of Auguste Jean Jacques Hervieu, painted a set of transparencies for a background setting. Powers created the wax figures and mechanical devices. Dorfeuille reaped the profits.

Based upon the literary models of Dante's *Divine Comedy* and Milton's *Paradise Lost,* "the Regions" featured an assortment of wax figures, some human in appearance, some animal, some a composite of both. All were grotesque. These figures were set in a spectral environment simulating Hell, or, actually, two Hells—one "hot," one "cold"—both of which were filled with meticulously fashioned, wild-eyed wax figures. One of the most effective figures in the cold Hell was an old Negro who was shown in the process of freezing to death. As the Museum handbill noted, it was a sad fate "for one so constitutionally fond of a warm climate."

Dominating the scene were some key characters. Near the entrance a wax female figure titled "Sin" periodically sprang toward the customers while emitting a horrid cry. Other "greeters" were "Minos, the Judge of Hell," Lucifer, "Belzebub" [*sic*], and "Cerberus" (the dog) and "Python" (the snake), the "Guardians of Hell." Somewhat to the rear of the exhibit stood a skeleton holding a standard which read:

To this grim form, our cherished limbs have come,
And thus lie mouldering in their earthly home;
In turf bound hillock, or in sculptured shrine,
The worms alike, their cold caresses twine;
So far we all are equal, but once left,
Our mortal weeds, of vital spark bereft,
Asunder, farther than the poles were driven;
Some sunk in deepest Hell, some raised to highest Heaven.

In the center of the exhibit, with smoke swirling about him, sat the "King of Terrors," dressed in his customary costume of red tights, red horns, forked tail, and holding a pitchfork. As the spectators cautiously entered the darkened attic—the exhibit was open only in the evening and could accommodate from thirty to forty patrons—the King (or Devil) warmly welcomed them to his realm and called their attention to the sign over the entrance: "Whoever enters here leaves hope behind." In the early years the King of Terrors was a human being, not a wax figure. The puckish Powers assumed the role. After a few years he tired of this nightly chore and automated the figure. Powers occasionally played another character role, the "Evil One." Adorned in a dark robe (the front of which featured a skull and crossbones), with a lobster's claw fixed on his nose, Powers glided through "the Regions." His main objective was to frighten the patrons; he was eminently successful. One of his favorite antics was to appear suddenly out of the dark and inquire nonchalantly of a petrified rustic: "Don't you smell sulphur?"[35]

From its inception "the Regions" underwent constant refinement. Expediency dictated the initial change. The crowds which thronged the exhibit room when "the Regions" first opened came to represent a serious problem. Some patrons began to finger the delicate wax models. Dorfeuille instructed Powers to devise a technique whereby the "Great Beast" could be restrained. The mechanical wizard quickly effected a solution. While performing as the King of Terrors, he held in his hand a wand which was connected to a "friction machine." When someone reached in to fondle a figure, Powers administered a galvanic jolt. In time he constructed an iron grating which separated the patrons from the exhibit, and woe to the unsuspecting whose hand penetrated the barrier. Dorfeuille's handbill, which had been written by Mrs. Trollope, explained in mystical phraseology the awful doom await-

[35] A hilarious account of Powers' activities as an actor in "the Regions" is provided in a letter from John Locke (of Cincinnati) to Powers, Aug. 15, 1852, Powers Papers, Box 2. A considerable number of the letters written by Cincinnatians to Powers when he was residing in Florence, Italy, allude to his career at the Museum. These letters suggest that Cincinnatians regarded Powers as a mechanical genius.

ing any mortal rash enough to approach the mysteries of the nether world too closely: "The proprietor would caution the visitors against putting their hands within the grating of this awful exhibition as the punishment for such temerity would not only be instantaneous but most shocking."

Dorfeuille may have reaped the profits from "the Regions," but all Cincinnati knew that the entertainment was basically Hiram Powers' creation. Not only did Powers fashion the characters, but he also developed sound effects for the exhibit. Each evening the Museum emitted a continuous clamor of shrieks and groans, the clanking of chains, the crash of thunder, the hissing of serpents, and assorted other sounds designed to terrorize the weak at heart. Powers himself confessed in later years that the "unearthly sounds" made his "own flesh creep."[36] Complementing the wax figures and sound effects were Hervieu's artistic transparencies which provided a fitting backdrop for the exhibit; they depicted scenes from Dante's Purgatory and Paradise.

During his six-year curatorship, Powers automated almost every figure in the display and added other mechanical refinements, making "the Regions" the most celebrated chamber of horrors in the country. With pardonable pride, Dorfeuille's handbill crowed: "This is the only exhibition of the kind in the United States." Foreign visitors were as greatly impressed by the spectacle as domestic viewers.[37] In her typically

[36] Powers to Sam Smith, Aug. 7, 1866, *ibid.*, Box 4. Powers also devised a lighting system whereby he could simulate the flash of lightning. The usual technique was to throw the exhibit area into total darkness, then issue a flash of lightning.

[37] Practically every European visitor who published a travel account made reference to the Museum and "the Regions." On the whole, they liked the Museum. There was mixed reaction to "the Regions," some judging it to be vulgar, others calling it an amusing and entertaining spectacle. Especially interesting are the travel accounts of Basil Hall, William Bullock, Harriet Martineau, C. F. Volney, Fredrika Bremer, and Michel Chevalier.

florid prose style, Mrs. Trollope described, and rendered her judgment on, "the Regions" in these words:

He [Dorfeuille] has constructed a pandaemonium in an upper story of his museum, in which he has congregated all the images of horror that his fertile fancy could devise; dwarfs that by machinery grow into giants before the eyes of the spectator; imps of ebony with eyes of flame; monstrous reptiles devouring youth and beauty; lakes of fire, and mountains of ice; in short, wax, paint, and springs have done wonders. "To give the scheme some more effect," he makes it visible only through a grate of massive iron bars, among which are arranged wires connected with an electrical machine in a neighbouring chamber; should any daring hand or foot obtrude itself within the bars, it receives a smart shock, that often passes through many of the crowd, and the cause being unknown, the effect is exceedingly comic; terror, astonishment, curiosity, are all set in action, and all contribute to make "Dorfeuille's Hell" one of the most amusing exhibitions imaginable.[38]

Steamboat travelers carried tales of "the Regions" throughout the West. It was effective word-of-mouth advertising. When packets docked in Cincinnati, those passengers not intent on drinking the taverns dry along the Public Landing dashed to the Museum between the loading and unloading of cargo. An occasional closing of "the Regions" was a newsworthy item and was duly reported in local papers.

When farmers from the Cincinnati hinterland came to the city they made it a point to visit "Dorfeuille's Hell" and get a foretaste of doom. If some sophisticated eastern visitors regarded the exhibit as "impious humbug," "disgraceful mummery," and "trumpery,"[39] local residents viewed it as one of the wonders of the world.

Local ministers, in particular, heartily approved of "the Regions," since the exhibit apparently had a salu-

[38] *Domestic Manners*, ed. Smalley, 62–63.
[39] See, for example, Charles Fenno Hoffmann, *A Winter in the West* (New York, 1835), II, 134–36.

tary effect on church attendance and could be effectively utilized in sermons and appeals for tithes. With customary shrewdness, Dorfeuille admitted ministers to the exhibit free of charge; his newspaper advertisements repeatedly stressed the theme that it was designed for "good moral and religious purposes." Parents frequently took their children to "the Regions" to point out to them the ultimate residence of incorrigible youth.

The popularity of "the Regions" notwithstanding, Dorfeuille began to sustain financial reverses by the mid-1830's.[40] There were inherent difficulties in operating the Museum at a profit on a twelve-month basis. When the river level fell during the summer months, the packet traffic, the source of many customers, also dried up. Protracted cold spells during the winter months also knocked business "into a cocked hat," especially if the Ohio River froze over.[41]

The loss of Powers in 1834 was a major disaster for Dorfeuille. With his departure for Washington, the mechanical efficiency of "the Regions" could not be maintained and the automated specimens deteriorated.[42]

His successor, Linden Ryder, another young Cincinnati artist of considerable promise, lacked his mechanical skill. In 1836 he informed Powers of all the repairs he had to make on the automated figures and concluded: "So frequently have these attentions been necessary that many a time and oft I have wished you in Hell rather than myself."[43] Ryder candidly acknowledged his mechanical shortcomings. It is interesting to note that Charles Bulfinch, Jr., a resident of Washing-

[40] Not even the strong editorial puffs of local newspapers and periodicals could provoke the local citizens to flock into the Museum. See, for example, *Buckeye and Cincinnati Mirror*, V (Nov. 14, 1835), 23.

[41] Ryder to Powers, Jan. 10, 1837, Powers Papers, Box 4; Dorfeuille to Powers, Feb. 17, 1835, *ibid.*, Box 1.

[42] Ryder to Powers, Dec. 23, 1835, *ibid.*, Box 4.

[43] Ryder to Powers, May 22, 1836, *ibid.*, Box 2.

ton, D.C., and son of the famous architect of the United States Capitol, sought Powers' assistance in securing his former position on the Museum staff. So eager was Bulfinch to get the job that he offered to work for $100 less than the salary Dorfeuille normally paid.[44] The appointment did not materialize. In a letter to Powers shortly after he left the Museum, a Cincinnati friend posed this riddle: "Why is Mr. Dorfeuille like a paradox?" He also supplied the answer: "Because he is not important although he has lost his Powers!"[45]

The traditional explanation for Powers' departure for Washington, D.C.—and subsequently, Florence, Italy, where he achieved a reputation as the Praxiteles of the nineteenth century and the "first sculptor of the age"—is that he was intent upon following a career as a sculptor. A considerable body of evidence, including Powers' own correspondence, supports this theory. In later years, however, Powers told an interviewer that he had left the Museum for two reasons. First, Dorfeuille reneged on a promise to make him a part-owner, and then he had been shortchanged on his salary: "He knew I kept no accounts; but he did not know that I reported all the money he gave me to my wife, who did keep our accounts. He tried to cheat me; but I was able to baffle him through her prudence and method."[46]

In 1839, the scientist-showman, Dorfeuille, sold his holdings for $6,500 to a group in Cincinnati, but retained the wax figures, some of his more sensational curiosities, and the main characters of "the Regions" and carted them off to New York City, where he opened a museum on Broadway at a site next to the American Museum.[47] He raised the price of admission to 50 cents, but continued the practice of free admission to members of the clergy. Dorfeuille's new venture contained a

[44] Bulfinch, Jr., to Powers, May 25, 1835, *ibid.*, Box 1.
[45] John King to Powers, March 8, 1835, *ibid.*, Box 2.
[46] Bellows, "Seven Sittings with Powers," *Appleton's Journal*, Sitting 3, in *ibid.*, Box 4.
[47] Ryder to Powers, March 15, 1839, *ibid.*, Box 4.

number of skeletons which he advertised as the remains of malefactors executed in Ohio during the preceding twenty years. Whether in Cincinnati or New York City, for Dorfeuille, the show "must go on." Within a year tragedy struck twice. First, his museum was destroyed by fire, and "the Regions" suffered a symbolically fitting end. On July 23, 1840, Dorfeuille died at the age of forty-nine.

The final years of the Western Museum can be summarized quickly. From 1839 to 1867, when it dissolved, the Museum languished as a center of hokum under a number of owners. Operating on the premise that one should not tamper with success, the new owners "restocked" the "Regions." A rival museum in Cincinnati also established one,[48] so local citizens and river travelers now had an opportunity to go to "Hell" twice on the same night, if they so desired.

In 1861 an Englishman named Edward Hingston accompanied his friend, the noted American humorist and showman Artemus Ward, on a visit to the Museum. Hingston's subsequent account of his visit constitutes the most graphic description of the Museum in its final years.[49] He found it to be a "very dingy, unattractive place" externally. "There were a few dirty bills posted about the entrance; there were the ruins of a hand-organ sending forth doleful sounds inside; there was a dingy light burning in the passage, and there appeared to be a most plentiful supply of dirt and dust in the interior, judging from the samples furnished at the very entrance." A Mr. Allen was then the proprietor.

Hingston's suspicions of the interior appearance proved to be correct. The lower floor was filled with curiosities: broken models; stuffed pigs; rusty swords and guns, remnants of the celebrated Battle of Tippecanoe; Indian artifacts; oddly shaped stones; a thunderbolt which "had been seen to fall in Kentucky";

[48] Franks' Museum had an exhibit called "Hellas Regions."
[49] *Genial Showman*, i, 24–40.

fragments of temples from the ruins of Sodom and
Gomorrah—so the caption read. Hingston added: "All
were foul with dust and begrimed with the soot of
lamps. An odour of mustiness seemed to emanate from
every object, and something suggested the idea of ugly
spiders being concealed in every cranny and crevice."

In the apartment above, Hingston noted improvement. The plumage of the stuffed birds, which probably
had been the work of Audubon, still retained some of
the original coloring. He did observe that the scales of
the "Horrid Alligator of the Amazon" were "more polished than they ever had been in the slime of its native
river." Many a westerner's hand apparently had
smoothed the alligator's hide. In glass cases along the
rear wall were the curiosities "preserved in spirits."
Still on exhibit, and conspicuously so, were the head
and hand of the murderer, Hoover. (One wonders what
happened to his heart!)

The waxworks exhibit was a disappointment to
Hingston. "There is no really good wax-work collection
in the United States," he wrote. "Were the executors of
Madame Tussaud to send over the Baker-Street one
just as it is, and arrange to show it a month or two in
one city, and then a month or two in another, they
would rapidly make a fortune." Ward, an inveterate
practical joker who was familiar with the Museum
from past visits, lamented the fact that he could not get
the cases open, for he felt a powerful urge to "take off
General [George] Washington's head and put it on the
shoulders of Queen Victoria."

An attendant, who recognized Ward from his past
visits, approached the men and remarked in an
apologetic tone:

"All the same, gentleman—all the same. We are scass
of anything new. General Fremont is the last; but
thar's a mistake in the figger. He's not such a whaler of
a man as that; but we had nothing else to spare."

"Whose body have you used for him?" asked Ward.

"It's the Emperor of Russia's. We'd done with him, and the varmints had got into his clothes."

Ward and the attendant then reminisced and chuckled heartily over the celebrated episode of the Queen of Sheba, described by Hingston as "a dirty wax figure, dressed in very tawdry robes of coloured muslin, and adorned with a large quantity of cheap Connecticut or Massachusetts jewels." The Queen was poised in a bending position, offering gifts of diamond rings and gold snuffboxes to King Solomon. As the attendant explained the episode to Hingston, Museum officials one day were mystified to see the gifts fall from the Queen's hands to the floor over and over again. The attendants maintained an intensive watch, replacing the objects each time, but to no avail. Suddenly they noticed that the Queen's body was shaking, then the arm. The offerings dropped to the floor once more. "We were a bit skeart," explained the attendant, "for she was awful nervous. I saw her shake all over as if she had the chills and fevers." When the Museum closed for the day, the apprehensive attendants "undressed" the Queen, and "thar in her stomach, and half way up her arm," they found a "cussed" snake. Two mysteries were now solved. Earlier, the Museum had featured an exhibit of live South American snakes. One disappeared. An exhaustive search had failed to disclose its place of concealment until now—the snake had made the Queen of Sheba its home.

It was drawing near to the time for "the Regions" show to begin. Hingston, Ward, and a dozen other patrons slowly made their way up a steep, "narrow, dirty and rickety" staircase. The Englishman was struck by the incongruity of moving up and the *"facilis descensus Averni"* of his "school-day reading, though I might have remembered that Dante, *'in mezzo del cammin,'* climbed a steep hill, meeting a panther, a lion, and a she-wolf on the way, before he had the good-fortune to fall in with Virgil, and accept his escort to the World of punishment." Entering the gloomy gallery, he noted the heavy bars and, behind them and below the surface of the gallery, "the Regions." The scene brought back memories of a visit he once had made to a church on the European continent. The church had contained two transparencies, one of Paradise, the other of Pandemonium. The resident priest used the transparencies in his lectures to children to illustrate the joys of Heaven and the tortures of Hell. When discussing Heaven, he pushed a lever, thereby increasing the light behind the transparency. He repeated the process when discoursing on Hell, and the children viewed darting flames and writhing sinners. "Had that good priest visited the city of Cincinnati, and gone to the exhibition of *The Infernal Regions*," wrote Hingston, "he would possibly have wished to barter for it his Pandemonium, and been willing to throw the Paradise into the bargain."

On the basis of Hingston's description, it would appear that an effort had been made to duplicate the general features of "the Regions" of the Dorfeuille era. Most of the old inhabitants were in the pit:

demons, fiends, serpents, dragons, skeletons, hobgoblins, and animals of forms more fearfully fantastic than any which Mr. Hawkins has figured as inhabiting a hypercarbonized earth in pre-adamite times. The face of each figure was turned towards us, and the mouth of each dragon or serpent was wide open. Nearer to the bars than any of the other figures was something not quite an elephant or hippopotamus, though its body resembled that of one of those animals; its face was more like that of a lion, while its tail was one of those wondrous structures one might fancy in a dream after a supper of raw pork—one which no comparative anatomist would have the hardihood to classify among the tails of things living, or that have lived. There was another monster, with something like the body of a bull and the head of a satyr. The artist probably intended it for the Minotaur of ancient Crete. Oddest of all the figures was that of the Genius of Evil himself, with the orthodox tail and hoof, but with horns of unnecessary length, and eyes of disproportionate magnitude. In his right hand he carried a pitch-fork, while with his left hand he supported his tail, so as to expose to view its barbed extremity.

Some spectators appeared terrified, indicating that this was their first visit. Others were obvious *habitués* since they remained composed and commented know-ingly:

"Thar's Old Nick; you'll see him presently; he's awful good."

"That's the Old Sarpent; wait a bit, he'll skear you."

"I reckon you'll like the raging Lion; he's like all fury—he's like all fury—he is."

Suddenly the lights were reduced to the point of total darkness. A few patrons screamed. The "knowing ones howled to terrify the timid a little more." A gong sounded. This was accompanied by roars and groans. The lights brightened and the figures in the pit, hereto-fore stationary, became a symphony of motion:

the serpents began to crawl, each of them thrusting out a large tongue; the skeleton commenced to glide along a railway laid down upon the floor; and, as it approached the bars of the gallery, to raise the right arm and shake the spear held in its hand. The winged demons flapped their goblin wings, radiant with tinsel and vampire-like in form; the gentleman in black made his way towards the bars with noiseless step, thrust his pitchfork towards the audience, twisted the barb of his tail up to the height of his head and shook a claw-like hand in the faces of three of the more youthful visitors who had taken front places close against the bars, and who did not seem to be in the least afraid.

Shades of Hiram Powers' creations!

One of the aforementioned youngsters called out the climactic rite of the grotesque exhibition: "Now for the Ragin Lion! his dander's risin!" A strange "hybrid monster" began to move its eyes, lash its tail, and turn its head. A loud roar, and shrieks and yells filled the room. Gongs sounded. Chains rattled. There was the roll of a muffled drum and a bloodcurdling Indian war whoop.

With the audience supposedly in a state of terror—not all were—it was time for moral instruction. "Lucifer" addressed the group, as in the days of Dorfeuille, with deep moral purpose. He cautioned them to behave properly or he would claim them at a future time. "I shall hev to hev you," he said. As he spoke, the three brazen youths sought "to jerk some pea-nuts through the eye-holes of the mask." Lucifer retaliated by poking his pitchfork at them. The Raging Lion ponderously came to the assistance of his "fellow fiend" and the "shower of pea-nuts became fierce and furious."

"It's young haythen yez are, ivery one of ye," groaned the Lion in a heavy brogue. "Ye don't reverince the divil yourself, and ye wont allow the ladies and gintlemen to. Ah, get out wid ye!"

One of the youths took careful aim and tossed a handful of peanuts between the jaws of the Raging Lion, causing him to cough violently. The boys were convulsed with laughter. Then a hand emerged from the Lion's mouth and grasped one youth's arm which had been "incautiously" placed too far within the bars. Fellow fiend Lucifer violently cuffed the young culprit while he was being held. "The Regions" was in uproar.

The lights were extinguished in the pit and turned up in the gallery. The show was over. There was a rush for the stairs. Ward advanced to the grating and threw a silver coin into the Lion's mouth. The Lion responded: "Thanks, yer honour. It's the likes of ye should come ivery night to the raygions." As they left the Museum, Ward voiced a sentiment which had been expressed countless times for over thirty years: "It's the best show in Cincinnati." Hingston acknowledged that "nothing we ever had in London could equal the entertainment provided for the visitor to the Ohio show-shop."

"The Regions" still held a fascinating appeal, but the glory days were over for the Museum. The novelty had worn off, and the vagaries of museum management were too great for a successful and sustaining operation. The end finally came in 1867. The Museum was "smashed up" and the collections were put up for auction. The fabled components of "the Regions" were sold by lot at very low prices. "Devils were at a discount. Pitchforks were not in demand. Demons of all kinds went for a song. Even old Satan himself brought only a dollar and a half!"[50] The musty, once-valuable scientific collections and the remaining curiosities were scattered; their whereabouts are unknown today.

The effect of the Museum upon the scientific development of Cincinnati and the West is impossible to measure. Daniel Drake's dream of having the Museum become the focal point for western scientific activities failed to materialize. Nor did it become a scientific center for the local academicians and dilettantes. These men banded into a new scientific association, the Western Academy of Sciences, in 1835 and did not maintain an active relationship with the Museum.

Whatever its failings as a promoter of serious scientific endeavor, the Museum did represent the first organized effort to advance the study of natural history and basic science in the middle West. Certainly, through exhibits and lectures, it transmitted rudimentary scientific concepts to the masses and made science palatable to them. Dorfeuille's competitor also aided in the popularization of science. Mrs. Trollope paused in her celebrated literary laceration of Cincinnati to interject this compliment on both museums: "Cincinnati has not many lions to boast, but among them are two museums of natural history; both of these contain many respectable specimens, particularly that of Mr. Dorfeuille, who has, moreover, some highly interesting Indian antiquities."[51]

Another positive jugment on the Western Museum alone was rendered by the learned Timothy Flint, who

[50] Sol Smith, *Theatrical Management* (New York, 1868), 267; see also, *Cincinnati Commercial*, July 2, 1867.
[51] *Domestic Manners*, ed. Smalley, 62.

spent some years in residence in Cincinnati: "Dorfeuille's museum is a rich study for the naturalist. The
number of specimens of minerals, fossils, and quartzs
is very great. . . . Everything is scientifically arranged, according to the new nomenclature."[52] It would
be proper to assume that the displays of the Western
Museum sharpened the awareness of local residents on
the nature and character of the natural and physical
history of the Ohio Valley.

Above all, the Museum afforded vicarious pleasure to
a generation of travelers, localites, and countless thousands of rustics from the Cincinnati hinterland, whose
conception of urban life was colored by their experience of visiting this wonderland. One can imagine the
sense of anticipation felt by an entertainment-starved
"country customer" after he perused Dorfeuille's
poetic advertisement:

> Come hither, come hither by night or by day,
> There's plenty to look at and little to pay;
> You may stroll through the rooms and at every turn
> There's something to please you and something to learn.
> If weary and heated, rest here at your ease,
> There's a fountain to cool you and music to please;
> And further, a secret I still have to tell,
> You may ramble up-stairs, and on earth be in ----.[53]

William Henry Venable, the eminent nineteenth-
century cultural historian of the Ohio Valley, grew up
on a farm north of Cincinnati. As a child, he once
visited the Museum. In later years, he wrote these
telling words:

The coarse extravagance of the Western Museum,
though revolting to taste, was redeemed by broad
humor which everybody could enjoy. The exhibition
was certainly wonderful, and it helped to sustain the
illusion that the City was a strange, unreal world, alto-
gether unlike the Country. My childish fancy confused
the living men and women swarming along the street

[52] *Western Magazine and Review*, I (1827), 79.
[53] Dorfeuille repeatedly placed this advertisement in Cincinnati newspapers.

with the lifelike wax-figures in the showcases. The unearthly, and by no means heavenly music, ground by hand from a peculiar big organ just within the entrance, haunted my ears like a ghost of lugubrious sound. The fat and talkative old French lady, who sat at the foot of the stairway to take our tickets, seemed as much a part of the mechanism of the place as were the grind-organ by the door and the moving skeletons in the Shades above.[54]

As indicated by Venable's words, in the context of nineteenth-century life the Western Museum assumed an importance that no modern museum can hope to achieve. During the period of Dorfeuille's ownership it was the most significant entertainment site in the Middle West and enjoyed a national reputation. Its total life represents an important footnote to the history of western science, entertainment, and hokum.

[54] "Going Down to Cincinnati," 137.

Joseph Henry's Conception of the Purpose of the Smithsonian Institution

Wilcomb E. Washburn

BY the terms of a will written in 1826, James Smithson, natural son of the Duke of Northumberland, bequeathed over half a million dollars to the United States of America to found in Washington "an establishment for the increase and diffusion of knowledge among men." Knowledge of his will came first to the attention of our chargé d'affaires in London, Aaron Vail, upon the death of the contingent residuary legatee, Smithson's nephew, Henry James Hungerford, in 1835. On July 28, 1835, Vail wrote the Secretary of State, giving details of the bequest and further commenting, "The caption of the Will is in language which might induce a belief that the Testator labored under some degree of mental aberration at the time it was made, tho' I understand that its allegations are not destitute of probability, at least."[1] Other observers were similarly at a loss to explain why Smithson had made such an unusual gift and why he had chosen the United States to be the recipient. Only the scholarly John Quincy Adams took Smithson at his word. As he put it in his diary entry for January 10, 1836, "So little are the feelings of others in unison with mine on this occasion, and so strange is this donation of half a million of dollars for the noblest of purposes,

[1] Dispatch 197 from Aaron Vail to Forsyth, July 28, 1835, Vol. 43, Record Group 59, General Records, Department of State, National Archives, Washington, D.C. The reference to the caption of the will, in which Smithson describes his parentage, is puzzling; perhaps Vail did not find his claims to "noble" birth believable.

that no one thinks of attributing it to a benevolent motive."[2]

President Adams, who had recommended a program of government support of culture and learning in his first annual message to Congress in December 1825, had failed utterly at that time to move a society absorbed in the material exploitation of the vast resources of the continent. In the Smithson bequest, the old aristocrat, now a member of Congress from Massachusetts, saw the opportunity to accomplish by a private benefaction what the government seemed unwilling to do as a matter of public policy.

The story of the ten-year fight Adams made to preserve the integrity of the will and of the honor of the United States has been told elsewhere.[3] Evolving from the long debate on Smithson's will came, on August 10, 1846, "An act to establish the 'Smithsonian Institution' for the increase and diffusion of knowledge among men." The act provided for the erection of a "suitable building" to house "objects of natural history, including a geological and mineralogical cabinet; also a chemical laboratory, a library, a gallery of art, and the necessary lecture rooms." It gave the direction of the Institution to a Board of Regents drawn from the executive, legislative, and judicial branches of government, as well as from private life, who were to make from the interest of the Smithson bequest "an appropriation, not exceeding an average of twenty-five thousand dollars annually, for the gradual formation of a library composed of valuable works pertaining to all depart-

[2] Adams' diary entry for Jan. 10, 1836, as extracted from *The Memoirs of John Quincy Adams*, ed. Charles Francis Adams (Philadelphia, 1876), and printed in William J. Rhees, ed., *The Smithsonian Institution: Documents Relative to Its Origin and History* (Smithsonian Miscellaneous Collections, XVII; Washington, D.C., 1880), 764.

[3] *The Great Design: Two Lectures on the Smithson Bequest by John Quincy Adams*, ed. with an introduction by Wilcomb E. Washburn and a foreword by L. H. Butterfield (Washington, D.C.: The Smithsonian Institution, 1965).

ments of human knowledge.[4]

Nothing was said in the bill about supporting original researches or publishing scholarly works, although the Regents were authorized to make use of any other moneys that might be available "as they shall deem best suited for the promotion of the purpose of the testator." Congress' specific legislative interpretation of the will of Smithson was confined to the provisions for a library, museum, art gallery, and lecture rooms. It was at this point that the figure of Joseph Henry emerged, and with Henry, an interpretation of Smithson's will that has only a tangential relationship to the interpretation of Congress. To Henry, the will could be interpreted in only one way. The primary obligation of those carrying out the will must be the "increase of knowledge." Dependent upon and subservient to that increase lay the requirement to "diffuse" the knowledge—"thus increased"—among men.[5] The two functions were not coordinate and equal; one was primary and the other operative only following the successful accomplishment of the other.

Joseph Henry's every decision during his tenure as Secretary of the Smithsonian Institution, from 1846 to 1878, was governed by his famous "Programme," which he caused to be reprinted in every annual report issued during his administration. On September 6, 1846, three months before his own appointment as Secretary, Henry drafted an answer to a letter of Alexander Dallas Bache, Henry's good friend and one of the Regents of the Smithsonian, "asking my opinion as to the meaning of the will and a plan of realizing the intention of the donor." In reply, Henry wrote:

The object of the institution is the increase and diffusion of knowledge. The increase of knowledge is much

[4] William J. Rhees, ed., *The Smithsonian Institution: Documents Relative to Its Origin and History, 1835–1899* (Washington, D.C., 1901), I, 429–34.

[5] Henry's "Programme of Organization of the Smithsonian Institution," introduction. The major portion of the plan was approved by the Board of Regents on Dec. 13, 1847.

more difficult and in reference to the bearing of this institution on the character of our country and the welfare of mankind much more important than the diffusion of knowledge. There are at this time thousands of institutions actively engaged in the diffusion of knowledge in our country, but not a single one which gives direct support to its increase. Knowledge such as that contemplated by the testator can only be increased by original research which requires patient thought and laborious and often expensive experiments. There is no civilized country in the world in which less encouragement is given than in our own to original investigations and consequently no country of the same means has done and is doing so little in this line. A person who has distinguished himself in England by original discoveries is certain of a reward—he is either preferred to some office under government, or to a living in the church if he has taken orders, or a fellowship in the University, or his name is placed on the pension list; or if he be very much distinguished he receives the honor of Knighthood, and in all cases he has the result of his labors secured to him by an international copyright, which prevents the free publication of foreign works. In France the person who devotes himself to science and succeeds in establishing a character for originality is elected a member of the National institute; receives from the government a salary during his life and is elected, if thought worthy a member of the Legion of Honor. These are powerful inducements to exertion in the way of original investigation entirely unknown in our country and some of them incompatible with the genius of our institutions. Indeed original discoveries are far less esteemed among us than their applications to practical purposes, although it must be apparent on the slightest reflection that the discovery of a new truth is much more difficult and important than any one of its applications taken singly. Notwithstanding the little encouragement given to original investigation among us, it is true something has been done but this is chiefly not in the line of science properly so called which is a knowledge of the laws of phenomena, but in that of descriptive natural history.[6]

[6] Henry to Bache, Sept. 6, 1846, Smithsonian Institution Archives, hereafter cited as SI Archives. For Henry's recollections concerning the circumstances relating to the letter of Sept. 6, 1846, see Henry to Prof. J. P. Lesley, June 12, 1877, *ibid.*

The Board of Regents, on September 8, 1846, resolved to appoint a committee of three "to digest a plan
to carry out the provisions of the act to establish the
Smithsonian Institution, and that they report the same
to the next meeting of the Board." The committee reported on December 1, but Henry's plan, so much at
variance with the will of Congress, was modified, re-
vised, and discussed for a full year before a final version, incorporating a compromise between the extreme
positions of Henry and the Congress, was reached.[7]

Nevertheless, Henry continued to believe, and to
argue, that

the only plan in strict conformity with the terms of the
Will, and which especially commended itself to men of
science, a class to which Smithson himself belonged,
was that of an active living organization, intended
principally to promote the discovery and diffusion of
new truths by instituting original researches, under
the direction of suitable persons, in History, Antiquities, Ethnology and the various branches of Physical
Science, and by publishing and distributing among libraries and other public institutions, accounts of the
results which might be obtained, as well as of those of
the labors of men of talent which could not otherwise
be given to the world.[8]

[7] *Report of the Organization Committee of the Smithsonian
Institution* (Washington, D.C., 1847), 5; William J. Rhees, ed.,
*The Smithsonian Institution: Journals of the Board of Regents,
Reports of Committees, Statistics, Etc.* (Smithsonian Miscella-
neous Collections, XVIII; Washington, D.C., 1880), 41. Different
versions of the plan were prepared; some are in the Smithsonian
Archives. One version, that sent to John Quincy Adams for his
comments, remains only in the copy in the Adams Papers.
Adams, *The Great Design*, ed. Washburn, where it is repro-
duced.

[8] Smithsonian Institution, *Annual Report of the Board of Regents for 1850*, 6–7. Since the annual reports of the Board of Regents and of the Secretary of the Smithsonian Institution have
often been printed in different ways with different pagination,
caution should be exercised in using the page numbers cited.
Since the reports are short, the references should not be difficult
to locate. Hereafter such references will be cited merely as
Annual Report.

Henry never ceased to point out that Smithson was "well acquainted with the precise meaning of words" and that, in the light of his own life of original scientific research, "there can be no reasonable doubt that he intended by the terms 'an establishment for the increase and diffusion of knowledge among men,' an institution to promote the discovery of new truths, and the diffusion of these to every part of the civilized world."[9]

Henry, in his private correspondence as well as in his public accounts, constantly stressed this definition of the famous words of Smithson.[10] In a letter to one friend, Henry showed one of his rare touches of humor:

I have been somewhat amused with the remarks of your friend, in reference to the "Congress of Lilliputian Savans" and Buncombe publications. You may inform him for me that although I prefer the Aristotelian to the Platonic philosophy, yet the Peripatetic scheme for the Smithsonian has never for a moment found favor with me, and I am equally averse to penny publications for the diffusion, among the many, of science falsely so called. The most prominent idea in my mind is that of stimulating the talent of our country to original research—in which it has been most lamentably difficient—to pour fresh material on the apex of the pyramid of science, and thus to enlarge its base. . . .

Though I have the highest respect for schools of practical science, yet my ideas of the Smithsonian tran-

[9] *Annual Report for 1856*, 18. Louis Agassiz reported that Smithson had already made his will, leaving his fortune to the Royal Society of London, when certain scientific papers that he submitted for publication to the society were turned down by it. Upon the refusal of that body to publish his papers he changed his will. Agassiz's letter is quoted in the speech of Rep. W. H. English, of Indiana, on the Smithsonian Institution in the House of Representatives, Feb. 27, 1855 (Rhees, ed., *Documents* [1901], I, 556). Agassiz's conclusion was that "nothing seems to indicate more plainly what were the testator's views respecting the best means of promoting science than this fact."

[10] See, for example, his letter to President Eliphalet Nott of Union College, Dec. 26, 1846, in *A Memorial of Joseph Henry* (Smithsonian Miscellaneous Collections, XVIII; Washington, D.C., 1880), 409.

scend even these. Practical science will always meet with encouragement in a country like ours. It is the higher principles—those, from which proper practice naturally flows that require to be increased and diffused. But since it will probably be found necessary to make a few oblations to Buncombe, practical science must have a share.[11]

Making oblations to Buncombe, i.e., Congress, was one of the prices Henry paid to gain his larger objectives. But as an economical man, Henry paid a very low price. He strove particularly to make Congress understand the difference between the increase and the diffusion of knowledge. As he put it in his *Report for 1859,*

At the beginning of this Institution the confusion of ideas on this subject was so great that in the interpretation of the will, even by some of our prominent and enlightened men, the diffusion of knowledge was identified with its increase; and it was contended that Smithson had used the terms as synonymous, and desired by the one merely to enforce the other. But that this was not the case may be gathered from the meaning attached to these terms by the class of men to which be belonged.[12]

On one occasion Henry even undertook to instruct the great Daniel Webster on Smithson's intention. Henry's daughter Mary recounted in her diary the story:

Webster listened in silence for some time and then replied that he believed Smithson had no such refined ideas when he used the term *increase* and *diffusion* of Knoledge he only meant by [them] to enforce his words. He then spoke rather disrespectfully of scientists in general. Father asked if he formed his opinion from the men of Cambridge and being annoyed at his manner let the deplomatist see that he at least deserved and demanded respect. He was sufficiently affable before the interview closed but Father entertained so disagreeable impression of his visit that he did not enter his presence again until compelled to do so.

[11] Draft of a letter from Henry to J. B. Varnum, June 22, 1847, SI Archives.
[12] P. 14.

Henry worked his magic on Webster, however, as he did on other legislators, and was able to convert the great orator to more "liberal views of science."[13]

Henry's position in enforcing his view of the true purpose of the Smithsonian was strengthened by his willingness and ability to resign. As the foremost American scientist of his day, numerous opportunities were open to him. The loss would be the Smithsonian's, not his. Princeton wished him to stay on or come back.[14] Harvard hoped that he would accept the Rumford chair which his Harvard friends assured him he could have for the asking.[15] But the finest opportunity was afforded by the vacancy, shortly after he assumed his Smithsonian position, of the chair of Dr. Robert Hare, at the University of Pennsylvania in Philadelphia. Both in terms of remuneration and research time, it was the best place for a scientist in America.[16]

In addition to the alternate positions Henry could choose from, his friends pointed out the positive disadvantages of the Smithsonian position. Charles Hodge, of Princeton, offered two particularly penetrating objections:

3. Is there any adequate security for the success or right conduct of an Institution under the control of Congress, in which that body have a right and will feel it to be a duty to interfere? Will it not be subject to party influences, and to the harassing questionings of coarse and incompetent men? Are you the man to have your motives and actions canvassed by such men as are to be found on the floor of our congress?
4. Is it an ascertained fact that either congress or public sentiment will sanction the proceedings of the

[13] Mary Henry's MS Diary, entry for Sept. 6, 1864, SI Archives; Henry to Bache, July 10, 1851, typescript copy by Mary Henry, *ibid*. The original letter is missing.

[14] Henry to Bache, Dec. 4, 1846, *ibid*.

[15] See, for example, draft of a letter from Henry to "My dear Sir," July 27, 1846, Asa Gray to Henry, Nov. 28 [1846], and Gray to Henry, Dec. 12, 1846, *ibid*.

[16] See, for example, R. A. Tilghman to Henry, Aug. 19, 1847, Henry to Bache, June 25, 1847, Henry to his brother James, July 10, 1847, *ibid*.

Regents in organizing the Institution on a plan so different from that obviously contemplated when the bill creating it passed congress?[17]

Another Princeton friend urged him to stay at Princeton, pointing out among other disadvantages the unjustified calls upon his time he would experience in Washington. "You will feel as I often did the pangs of regret attending the perfect waste of time upon persons who really have no claim upon you but whom you cannot repulse." Henry, in going over this correspondence at a later time, noted after this passage, "(How prophetic)."[18]

Since the Philadelphia offer came shortly after he had entered upon his duties as Smithsonian Secretary, Henry was reluctant to abandon his effort to put the Institution on a proper course, though sufficiently attracted by the Philadelphia offer to compare himself to "the ass between two bundles of hay." However, as in the case of the previous offers, the knowledge of the Philadelphia offer strengthened his hand with the Regents. As he wrote in a letter to his friend Bache, one of the Regents, in regard to his plan of organization, "I am resolved [it] shall not be interfered with by the ulterior objects of any individual of the board. I foresee therefore difficulties at the next meeting which may cause me to resign and could I calculate the moral future, under given circumstances, with as much precision as the physical, I could more easily determine my course in reference to the position in Philadelphia."[19]

Henry's cavalier attitude toward Congress can be explained in part by his rigid belief in the priority of the will of Smithson to that of Congress. As he put it at the end of his life, when recounting the objections that were at first raised to his plan, such as " 'that Congress has enacted laws in regard to the Institution, which

---

[17] Hodge to Henry, Dec. 5, 1846, *ibid.*
[18] N. B. Hope to Henry, Dec. 7, 1846, *ibid.*
[19] June 25, 1847, *ibid.*

11. The Smithsonian Institution, *ca.* 1862. Photograph by A. J. Russell.

12. Young Spencer Baird.

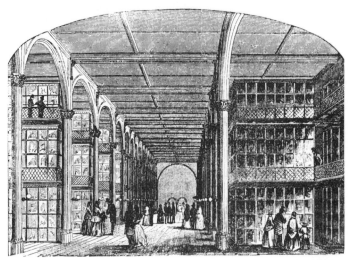

13. The Museum—now called the Great Hall of the original Smithsonian Building. Engraving from the early 1860's.

must be obeyed.' In reply to this I said: 'the resolutions of Congress may be changed, but the will of a dead man should be inviolable.' "[20]

The temptation to accept the Philadelphia chair must have been particularly great when Henry pondered the magnitude of the task ahead of him. After all, Henry was trying singlehandedly to reinterpret the will of Congress and make Congress like it! Not an easy task. At the same time a sudden resignation would suggest opportunism, an impression Henry bent over backward to avoid. Henry's friends attempted to relieve his fears on this point. R. A. Tilghman wrote reassuringly, "As to your being under any obligations to it [the Smithsonian] on account of your election thereto, I must beg of you not to trouble yourself in the least with any such idea. The benefit was on their side; they chose you because you were the best person they could find, and would not have done so had it been otherwise."[21]

Though sorely tempted, Henry declined to abandon the challenge he had taken up. In a letter to E. G. Squier, principal author of the first Smithsonian "Contribution to Knowledge," he wrote:

I presume on account of the articles in the newspapers relative to my resignation from the Smithsonian you are somewhat anxious to hear from me. Though I have been much tempted to accept the chair in Philadelphia particularly as a proposition was made by one of the Regents of the Smithsonian and agreed to by the leading members of the Trustees of the University, that I might retain the direction of the Institution, until it got fairly under way, the work being attended to by others, and accept the chair of chemistry. I found however this plan "impractical" and therefore resolved *sink* or *swim live* or *die* I would hold on to the Smithsonian. I consider that I have made a sacrifice for the cause of American science and though I may not succeed in rendering the Institution what it ought to be

[20] Henry to Prof. Lesley, Jan. 12, 1877, *ibid.*
[21] Tilghman to Henry, Aug. 19, 1847, *ibid.*

yet I shall at least deserve some credit for the attempt.[22]

The Building

Immediately upon his appointment as Secretary of the Smithsonian, Henry set out to rescue the Smithson bequest from those, in Congress and out, who had failed to comprehend the meaning of Smithson's will. His first concern was with the plan for a costly edifice, a building intended by Congress to provide a home for the specimens of natural history collected by the U.S. Exploring Expedition which, under Lieutenant Charles Wilkes, had made scientific investigations throughout the world in 1838–42. The collections were overflowing the U.S. Patent Office where they were housed and overwhelming the administrative capacity of the privately organized National Institution for the Promotion of Science (or National Institute, as it was later called) to which they had been entrusted.

Following his first meetings with the Board in December 1846, Henry optimistically wrote his wife:

I have succeeded beyond my most sanguine expectation in molding the opinions of the board of Regents into that of my plans but the difficulty is that we are hampered with the law of Congress which directs that a building shall be erected with rooms suitable to con[t]ain on a liberal scale objects of natural history and particularly the collection of the [Wilkes] exploring expedition. Now this collection is of such a size that it will require an immense building to contain them and this will absorb so much of the annual interest in the way of taking care of the collection that there will be but little left for the proper purposes of the Institution.[23]

Writing a few days later to Dr. Eliphalet Nott, President of Union College, Henry was even more em-

[22] July 3, 1847, Manuscript Division, Library of Congress, Washington, D.C.
[23] Dec. 22, [1846], SI Archives.

phatic. After stating that he had accepted the position at the solicitation of "friends of science in our country to prevent its falling into worse hands and with the hope of saving the noble bequest of Smithson from being squandered on chimerical or unworthy projects," Henry went on to assert that "unless I can succeed in changing the plan of erecting an immense building the funds of the bequest will be lost to all useful purpose." However, realizing that such a task might be too difficult even for himself, he crossed out the last sentence and substituted the more flexible statement: "Unless the Institution is started with great caution there is danger of absorbing all the income in a few objects when in themselves [sic] may not be the best means of carrying out the design."[24]

Henry's fear of "squandering" the Smithson fund on "bricks and mortar" or on "other unworthy objects" is a constant theme throughout his correspondence of the period, and though he was forced to compromise, his attitude expressed itself in a constant pressure on James Renwick, the architect, to build economically.[25]

To Henry it was obvious that "the plans and dimensions of the building should be determined by the plan of the organization, and not the converse."[26] Or, as he put it in a brilliant metaphor in his *Annual Report for 1856*, "It is surely better, in the construction of such an edifice, to imitate the example of the mollusc, who, in fashioning his shell, adapts it to the form and dimensions of his body, rather than that of another animal who forces himself into a house intended for a different occupant."[27] Though Henry conceded that the plan of

[24] Two drafts of letter to Nott, Dec. 26, 1846, *ibid.* Cf. the printed version, published as a note to the "Discourse of W. B. Taylor" on Henry, in *Memorial of Joseph Henry*, 409–10.

[25] Henry to "Dear sir," Dec. 11, 1846, SI Archives. A typical entry in Henry's 1849 desk calendar, for July 17, 1849, reads: "insisted on having ordinary scroles on the ends of the seats of the lecture room."

[26] From Henry's "Programme of Organization," quoted in *Memorial of Joseph Henry*, 400.

[27] P. 15.

the building as prepared by "young [James] Renwick
. . . is certainly beautiful," he was appalled at the
$202,000 price tag and expressed the hope of seeing the
wings chopped off. As he wrote to his wife, "Though I
am an admirer of good building yet I do not choose to
be its victim."[28]

Henry fought a determined battle to reduce the
amount to be spent for the building at the January
1847 meetings of the Board of Regents, threatening,
indeed, to resign if the plans went ahead as scheduled.[29]
Although he considered himself to "have on my side all
the best men," including the Vice President, Bache,
Chief Justice Taney, Judge Sidney Bresse, and probably General Lewis Cass, he acknowledged that the
other side was stronger. "Unfortunately," he complained, "[Robert Dale] Owen is struck with an architectural mania and were it not for this the builders
would be in the minority."[30] Bache was able to calm
Henry's anger by a compromise which delayed the construction of the building to allow for a greater accumulation of interest from the Smithson fund for what
both regarded as the true purpose of the Institution.
The compromise also automatically delayed the need to
consider the problem of taking charge of the museum
of the Wilkes Expendition. "Indeed," Henry wrote, "I
hope before the building is finished to see generally
acknowledged the gross injustice of putting the support of the museum of the government of the United
States on a small fund the bequest of a foreigner for
another object."[31]

Henry accepted the compromise with reluctance.
Writing to Bache in March 1847 from Princeton,
where he was finishing out the academic year, Henry
assured his friend that he could

look back if not with complacency on the norman ceno-
taph, at least with resignation and if the building *is* to

[28] Jan. 18, 1847, Jan. 20, 1847, SI Archives.
[29] Draft of letter from Henry to "Dear Sir," July 1, 1847, *ibid.*
[30] Henry to his wife, undated, calendared "? Dec. 1846?" *ibid.*
[31] Henry to his wife, Jan. 29, 1847, *ibid.*

be erected I can imagine much good may still be done with the remainder of the funds, though I have not changed my opinion of the impropriety of the measure which devotes so much of the bequest to a gratification of a sensuous kind and I still hope to see the building postponed or abandoned.[32]

Indeed, Henry never ceased to bemoan the great amount tied up in the turreted Norman pile which now serves principally as an "administration building" for the numerous Smithsonian museums and bureaus. In a letter to President Andrews of Kent College in 1856, Henry complained of the expense of the building and asserted that "if the Institution could give it away and be relieved from the support of a library and museum the Smithsonian bequest could be made to yield much more valuable fruit than it now does."[33]

In his *Annual Report for 1856,* Henry expressed the hope that

Congress would relieve the Institution from the care of a large collection of specimens principally belonging to the government, and purchase the building to be used as a depository of all the objects of natural history and the fine arts belonging to the nation. If this were done, a few rooms would be sufficient for transacting the business of the Institution, and a larger portion of the income would be free to be applied to the more immediate objects of the bequest. Indeed, it would be a gain to science could the Institution give away the building for no other consideration than that of being relieved from the costly charge of the collections.[34]

The Library

Perhaps the most logical direction in which the Smithsonian might have gone, but for Joseph Henry, was toward the creation of a great national library. The library scheme had figured prominently in the early

[32] March 30, 1847, *ibid.*

[33] Feb. 23, 1856, Doc. 78, Lorin Andrews Papers, Ohio Historical Society, Columbus, Ohio. I am indebted to Keith Melder for this reference.

[34] P. 17.

debates on the Smithsonian and had strong support on the Board of Regents as it was constituted in the early years.

Senator Rufus Choate of Massachusetts was the leading proponent of the library scheme, and his speech of January 8, 1845, on the subject would, in the opinion of a writer in the *North American Review,* "render more memorable the day on which it was delivered than that gallant military achievement of which it is the anniversary." Choate declared: "Does not the whole history of civilization concur to declare that a various and ample library is one of the surest, most constant, most permanent, and most economical instrumentalities to increase and diffuse knowledge? There it would be—durable as liberty, durable as the Union: a vast storehouse, a vast treasury, of all the facts which make up the history of man and of nature, so far as that history has been written.[35]

A more ingenious plea for the creation of a great library, and one which no doubt infuriated Henry, was made by the "versatile Vermonter," George Perkins Marsh, in a speech in the House of Representatives on April 23, 1846, just prior to its approval of the Smithsonian bill. As Marsh noted:

The purpose of the testator, which we are to carry out, was "the increase and diffusion of knowledge among men." What, then, is the most efficient means of increasing and diffusing knowledge? Increase, accumulation, must precede diffusion. Every rill supposes a fountain; and knowledge cannot "flow down our streets like a river," without there be first built and

[35] *The Smithsonian Institution: An Article from the North American Review* (Boston, 1854), 19; the reference is to the Battle of New Orleans, Jan. 8, 1815. Rhees, ed., *Documents* (1901), I, 287. In her comments on a letter of her father in which he disparaged oratory, particularly congressional oratory, Mary Henry noted that despite his remarks he delighted in eloquence, and that "of the great speech of Mr. Choat against the Institution he spoke always with great pleasure. He enjoyed it throughly although opposed so entirely to his views." Comment added to typed transcription of letter of Henry to his wife, May 1, 1847, SI Archives.

filled a capacious reservoir, from which those streams shall issue. It is an error to suppose that the accumulation of the stores of existing learning, the amassing of the records of intellectual action, does not tend also to *increase* knowledge. What is there *new* in the material world, except by extraction or combination?

Marsh's peroration made no concessions to experimental science:

But what are we offered instead of the advantages which we might hope to reap from such a library as I have described? We are promised experiments and lectures, a laboratory and an audience hall. Sir, a laboratory is a charnel house, chemical decomposition begins with death, and experiments are but the dry bones of science. It is the thoughtful meditation alone of minds trained and disciplined in far other halls, that can clothe these with flesh, and blood, and sinews, and breathe into them the breath of life. Without a library, which alone can give such training and such discipline, both to teachers and to pupils, all these are but a masqued pageant, and the demonstrator is a harlequin.[36]

Marsh's language may appear unduly offensive. But the context of the debate on the Smithsonian should be remembered. Robert Dale Owen of Ohio had, the previous day, ridiculed the proponents of a big library who sought "to rival the bibliomaniacs of Paris and of Munich." "Are there a hundred thousand volumes in the world worth reading?" Owen asked rhetorically, and answered "I doubt it much";

It grieves me not, that the fantastic taste of some epicure in learning may chance to find, on the bookshelves of Paris, some literary morsel of choice and ancient flavor, such as our own metropolis supplies not. I feel no envy, if we republicans are outdone by luxurious Europe in some high-seasoned delicacy of the pampered soul. Enough have we to console ourselves!—objects of national pride, before which these petty antiquarian triumphs dwarf down into utter

---

[36] Rhees, ed., *Documents* (1880), 422–23, 426. See the excellent biography of Marsh by David Lowenthal, *George Perkins Marsh: Versatile Vermonter* (New York, 1958).

insignificancy! Look abroad over our far-spreading land, then glance across to the monarchies of the Old World, and say if I speak not truth![37]

Owen's pet project, for which he thought the Smithsonian fund ideal, was to create a series of normal schools as a method of elevating the character of common school instruction. Such a purpose, Owen asserted, "I hold . . . to be a far higher and holier duty than to give additional depth to learned studies, or supply curious authorities to antiquarian research." To this proposal John Quincy Adams averred that he would rather have the whole sum of money thrown into the Potomac than to appropriate one dollar for that purpose.[38]

Henry, despite Congress' specific authorization for the creation of a large library, criticized the idea, conceding only that "a working library however is necessary for carrying out the plan we have proposed for increasing knowledge and hence a small part of the income of the institution should be annually expended in purchasing suitable books." Henry continued to think of the library as properly designed "for facilitating scientific research"—not as the nucleus of a national library.[39]

The Board of Regents, more sensitive to congressional wishes, informed Henry during the maneuvers leading to his appointment as Secretary that they already had a candidate for the position of assistant secretary in charge of the library, Charles Coffin Jewett. Born in Lebanon, Maine, in 1816, Jewett attended Dartmouth and Brown and then served as Librarian of Andover Theological Seminary. In 1841 he was appointed librarian of Brown University, and in 1843 he published a catalogue of the library. Soon thereafter he was elected professor of modern languages and literature at the university, in addition to his duties as li-

[37] Rhees, ed., *Documents* (1880), 374–75, 377.
[38] *Ibid.*, 379, 440.
[39] Henry to Bache, Sept. 6, 1846, SI Archives; Henry to John E. Gray, British Museum, June 13, 1849, John Edward Gray Papers, American Philosophical Society, Philadelphia.

brarian. On a sabbatical in Europe he spent two and a half years becoming familiar with the great libraries there, improving his command of languages, and buying books for the Brown library.[40]

Jewett's appointment was the only one at the Smithsonian made for Henry, and this fact was to have fateful consequences. Bache informed Henry that the Regents expected Jewett to be made assistant secretary in charge of the library, and, on December 5, 1846, before his own appointment, Henry wrote, "I shall also follow your advice in reference to the appointment of Professor Jewett. I think it proper as well as politic that this position should be filled by a man of letters rather than of science. On all other points I shall keep myself uncommitted."[41]

Later in December Professor Jewett passed through Princeton and visited Henry at his home. "I found him a very pleasant gentleman and had a long talk with him," Henry wrote, "gave him my views candidly and received from him an equally frank response. I think our views are so adverse that he will not accept the appointment. The salary is so small and the plan of the institution which I propose so different that we cannot agree."[42] Jewett later asserted that it was during this meeting at Princeton that he first learned of Henry's true feelings about the library, and that, although Henry urged him to remain as his assistant under his scheme, he "emphatically declined" and returned to Providence with the intention of abandoning all thought of connection with the Smithsonian. But he found others, he reported, who took a different view from that of Henry. "They thought it was dangerous to

[40] Biographical notice of Jewett by Reuben A. Guild, in Rhees, ed., *Journals*, 336–37.

[41] Henry to Bache, Dec. 5, 1846, SI Archives. The letter is in answer to Bache's letter of Dec. 4, 1846, to Henry, incomplete typed copy of the missing original of which, prepared by Mary Henry, is in *ibid*.

[42] Henry to his wife, undated, calendared "Dec. 27, 1846?" *ibid*.

attempt to change the law, and were sure that Professor Henry's plan could not be carried out under the law."[43]

When the Regents met in January of 1847, "Mr. Choate the great Library man whom I have not yet seen"—as Henry wrote—was at first absent but shortly appeared. At the January 26 meeting a compromise was agreed upon by which $15,000 was to be appropriated annually following the completion of the building to build up the library and museum collections, while the remainder of the annual interest was to be allotted to the preparation and publication of original researches and lectures. Following the approval of this "compromise,"

Mr. Choate and his friends stated, that they concurred in my appointment, with the understanding that the plan of a Library would not be entirely abandoned and that Prof. Jewett would be appointed my assistant. He further stated, that he had been informed, that I was not anxious to assume the responsibility of nominating the assistant and hoped that the Board would recommend to me Prof. Jewett—whereupon a majority of the Board recommended the gentleman and, in compliance with the recommendation, I appointed him.[44]

On seeing the minutes of the proceedings the following morning, Henry noted that the fact that the Board had "requested the nomination" of Jewett was omitted and insisted that it be stated in the minutes.[45] The Journal states, in somewhat different words from those Henry used, that the Regents requested the Secretary to "nominate to the Board an assistant who shall be the librarian, and whose salary [set by the Board at $2,000] shall commence whenever the building shall be

[43] U.S. Congress, House Select Committee on the Smithsonian Institution, *Report by Charles W. Upham, March 3, 1855* (Washington, D.C., 1855), 114–16.

[44] Henry to his wife, Jan. 20, 1847, SI Archives; Henry to his wife, Jan. 27, 1847, typescript prepared by Mary Henry; original letter missing, *ibid.* See the discussion of the episode in *Upham Report*, 100–101.

[45] Henry to his wife, Jan. 27, 1847, SI Archives.

ready for the reception of the library." The Journal
notes further that Henry, "understanding Professor
Charles C. Jewett, of Brown University, to be the
preference of a majority of the Board, he, therefore,
nominated Charles C. Jewett for Assistant Secretary,
acting as librarian, of the Smithsonian Institution."[46]
The Board approved the nomination.

Jewett's letter to Henry accepting the appointment
was brief and unenthusiastic. "I have," wrote Jewett,
"after due deliberation, concluded to accept the office."
Jewett later reported how surprised he was to receive
the offer, that his first inclination had been to decline
the appointment, but that conversation "with gentlemen interested in the library plan" had induced him to
accept.[47] Encouraged by the strong support in Congress
for a great library, Jewett may have tended—as Henry
charged—to regard his "office" as only nominally subor-
dinate to Henry. The supporters of the library scheme
on the Board of Regents encouraged the attitude.[48]

Choate obtained the appointment of a library committee of the Board which, on January 27, caused the
adoption of a resolution by the whole Board:

That the Assistant Secretary, acting as librarian, be
employed for the purposes specified in the foregoing
resolution [preparing book catalogues, purchasing
books on bibliography, collecting information on other
libraries, collecting books] *under the direction of a
committee of three members of the Board,* to be ap-

[46] Rhees, ed., *Journals*, p. 27. In his letter of Dec. 15, 1846, to
his wife (SI Archives), Henry assured her that the newspaper
stories that Jewett had been appointed at a salary of $3,000
were untrue; "the Regents will not think of giving him half of
this sum certainly not more." Henry's salary was $3,500 with
$500 additional allowance for a house until rooms were provided
for him in the Smithsonian building.

[47] Jewett to Henry, Feb. 11, 1847, printed in Rhees, ed., *Journals*, 34; *Upham Report*, 114–15.

[48] Senator Choate, for example, telegraphed "Professor Jewett" from Boston that he would be in Washington on the Monday
following. The Board, with what must have been an irritated
Henry in attendance, received the telegram during its meeting
of Dec. 17, 1847, and adjourned until the following Tuesday to
allow Choate to be present. Rhees, ed., *Journals*, 45.

pointed by the Chancellor, and to act *in conjunction with the Secretary*, at a compensation to be fixed by the Executive Committee, but not to exceed one thousand dollars, for any services he may render between this date and the time fixed for the commencement of his regular duties as Assistant Secretary.[49]

Choate, George Perkins Marsh, and Alexander D. Bache were appointed as the committee.

The undercutting of Henry's authority, even though the appointment preceded the regular entry of Jewett into his duties as assistant secretary, will be immediately apparent. Jewett subsequently commented, "It seems that Professor Henry was all the time under the influence of a feeling, that, in yielding to the direction of the Regents in nominating an assistant secretary to act as librarian, he had parted with a prerogative; and he seems to have been not less under the impression that some power over the other officers, which he might claim under the law, had been taken from him by the Regents."[50]

The dispute between Henry and Jewett led, in 1855, to the firing of the latter by the Secretary, Senator Choate's angry resignation from the Board of Regents, a congressional investigation, and, finally, the deposit of the bulk of the Smithsonian Institution library in the Library of Congress in 1866.[51] Jewett was an outstanding man, and his innovations as Smithsonian librarian were largely responsible for the development of the Library of Congress Catalog of Printed Cards as we know it today, the Union Catalog, and other reforms best known to the library profession. Jewett went on to make the Boston Public Library one of the great libraries of the country.[52] Henry encouraged Jewett's aggressive innovations in improving the scholar's

[49] *Ibid.*, 49. My italics.
[50] *Upham Report*, 118.
[51] See *ibid.* for a more complete account of the dispute.
[52] See Walter M. Whitehill, *The Boston Public Library: A Centennial History* (Cambridge, Mass., 1956); Joseph A. Borome, *Charles Coffin Jewett* (Chicago, 1951).

ability to know about and to find information of use to him. He refused, however, to build up a vast national library by spending the Smithson funds at the rate authorized by law despite the pressure of the "library" group in Congress and the urging of his Assistant Secretary. When, in 1868, Jewett died suddenly, and a biographical notice was included in the journals of the Board of Regents, a passage asserted that Jewett was "doomed . . . to disappointment in his efforts to build a great national library, and thus to carry out what he understood to be the expressed wishes of Congress in regard to the expenditure of the Smithsonian funds." Henry, at this point, inserted a note that "the wishes of Mr. Jewett in regard to a library at the seat of government worthy of the nation, are now being realized by the action of Congress, through the influence of the Smithsonian Institution, though not at the expense of its funds.—J. H."[53]

Henry was not against a great national library, but he felt its assembly and upkeep would dissipate the funds available to him and fail to accomplish the end set by the donor: the increase and diffusion of knowledge. As a Special Committee of the Board of Regents put it in 1854, "Neither of these purposes could be accomplished or materially advanced by the accumulation of a great library at the city of Washington. This would be to gather within the walls of a building here those fruits of learning which had been reaped elsewhere. It would be the *hiving* of knowledge, not its increase and diffusion."[54]

The friends of the library plan chose the wrong ground on which to argue their case: the ground of Smithson's intent. Henry, by the force of his character, eloquence, and administrative skill, had already occupied that ground, and had demonstrated his success in holding it against the varied attacks of his enemies.

[53] Rhees, ed., *Journals*, 337.
[54] *Ibid.*, 104 (Report of the Special Committee, May 20, 1854, Mr. J. Meacham not concurring).

The only hope of the library advocates was in demonstrating that Henry had failed to carry out the will of Congress. Had Senator Choate been willing to fight the battle actively in 1855, he might have succeeded in impressing this point of view upon his colleagues. But, discouraged, he left the battle to lesser men like Charles W. Upham, to whom he wrote from Boston regretting his inability to aid in the investigation, but suggesting the proper ground upon which it might focus:

It was never my purpose to do more than discuss the question of the intent of Congress. The intent of Smithson is not the problem now. It is the intent of Congress; and that is so transparent, and is so evidenced by so many distinct species of proof, that I really feel that I should insult the committee by arguing it. That Congress meant to devise a plan of its own is certain. The uniform opinion of men in Congress from the start has been that it must be so. Hence, *solely,* the years of delay, caused by the difficulties of devising a plan. Why not have at once made a Board, and devolved all on them? But who ever thought of such a thing? If, then, Congress would mean, and had meant, to frame a plan, what is it? Nothing, unless it is that of collections of books, specimens of art and nature, and possibly lectures. It is either these exactly, or it is just what the Regents please. But it cannot be the latter, and then it is these.[55]

Librarians never forgave Henry for his actions with regard to the Smithsonian library. Late in 1870, when Justin Winsor, the Librarian of the Boston Public Library, sought the assistance of Senator Charles Sumner in getting the Smithsonian to pay publication costs for a new edition of William Frederick Poole's *Index to Periodical Literature,* Sumner forwarded Winsor's letter to Joseph Henry for his opinion. Henry replied that the Institution's funds for the next few years were committed to other projects and he hoped another

[55] Samuel Gilman Brown, *The Life of Rufus Choate* (6th ed.; Boston, 1898), 161.

source of support could be found for Poole's book. When Poole saw Henry's letter, he commented:

> Prof. Henry's reasons are excellent. The second cannot be beaten: "the preparation of a new orbit for the planet Neptune"! The old one is probably worn out. Let the planet be supplied without delay with so proper an appendage. Without a proper orbit it may be butting against our planet, and disturbing generally to the order of the solar system. I hope you will have the letter published. The world ought to know what the "most useless" institution in creation is doing and proposing to do.[56]

The Museum

Henry eventually won his battle against making a national library of the Institution, but he was less successful in opposing its expansion into a full-scale museum. In September 1846, when Henry sat down and wrote the first draft of his famous program, the subject of a museum did not occupy a prominent position:

> Will the diffusion of knowledge be much promoted by a large expenditure of the income of the institution in the purchases of curiosities, minerals and other objects for the illustration of natural history? We think not; the influence of such a collection must also be local. The purchase should in the first place be limited to such objects as are more immediately important in the prosecution of any new branch of natural history, such as full sets of microscopic preparations for the use of those engaged in researches of this kind. A museum however may be gradually formed by a small annual appropriation for the purchase of new articles and the preservation of such specimens as may be presented.[57]

In the early meetings of the Board of Regents in January 1847, however, Henry was forced to compro-

---

[56] Poole to Winsor, Jan. 12, 1871, in Boston Public Library, quoted in William Landram Williamson, *William Frederick Poole and the Modern Library Movement* (New York, 1963), 46.

[57] Henry to Bache, Sept. 6, 1846, SI Archives.

mise on more than the building itself. As Henry put it in a letter to his wife, the Board of Regents

determined on the plan of organization today and adopted my plans in full so far as one half of the income was concerned—the other half they were obliged to give to the Library, the museum and other collections with the hope that if the Institution does well Congress will assist them by paying for the keeping of the museum. They could not get rid of the museum unless they went back with the institution to Congress and it was concluded that this would be a hasardous plan and could not be thought of this session.[58]

Henry's fear that the Smithson fund would be applied to the care of the national collections pulled him in two directions. On the one hand, it encouraged his personal inclination in the summer of 1847 to wash his hands of the Smithsonian and take the chair vacated by Dr. Hare at the University of Pennsylvania. On the other hand, this same fear, utilized by Henry's friends in an appeal to his spirit of self-sacrifice and honor, helped to impel him to a determination to save the Smithson bequest for its intended purpose. They argued "that my resignation at this time would be most disastrous to the establishment—that it would dwindle down into a mere hospital for Invalids and an *omnium gatherum* of all kinds of trash."[59]

Henry's decision to stay, and his adamant refusal to take on the responsibility of a national museum, was a disappointment to some. Titian Ramsay Peale, the artist of the Wilkes Exploring Expedition, wrote despairingly to friends in Philadelphia in the summer of 1848 that

I have communicated to Mr. Dallas [Vice President of the United States and Chancellor of the Board of Regents of the Smithsonian], and to Prof. Henry, my opinion that the collections of natural history made at the government expense, lean upon the Smithsonian

[58] Undated, calendared "? Dec. 1846?" *ibid.;* see also draft of letter from Henry to "Dear Sir," July 1, 1847, *ibid.*

[59] Henry to his brother James, July 10, 1847, *ibid.*

14. The Ethnology Department, Smithsonian Institution, early 1860's.

15. Osteology Department, Smithsonian Institution, *ca.* 1890.

Institution for support and preservation—It is a "broken reed."—but it makes me melancholy to desert my post, even when starved out.

Peale's hopes for the curatorship of the Smithsonian Museum were dashed: "the Smithsonians are opposed to a Museum," he sighed.[60]

Henry's views were categorical on this point: "Unfortunately the law of Congress obliges us to make provision for the great museum of the exploring expedition which will consume annually in the interest on the building and cost of keeping of the museum nearly if not quite the half of all our income. I consider this a gross misapplication of the funds. The bequest of Smithson was never intended to support the Museum of the United States."[61]

Congress' incorporation of a museum in its definition of the purposes of the Smithsonian was not entirely disinterested. The collections of specimens brought back by governmental exploring expeditions required more attention and space than they were receiving in their temporary patent office home. For the purpose, an elaborate building, such as that forced upon Henry by Congress, would provide an answer. Henry doggedly fought off the gift. As Professor Silliman of Yale wrote Henry, "If it is within the views of the Government to bestow the National Museum upon the Smithsonian Institution, the very bequest would seem to draw after it an obligation to furnish the requisite accommodations without taxing the Smithsonian funds: otherwise the gift might be detrimental instead of beneficial." Silliman's caution was repeated

[60] Peale to John Fries Frazer, July 3, 1848, Frazer Papers, American Philosophical Society.

[61] Portion of a letter to "Judge Lewis," Oct. 13, 1847, SI Archives. According to G. Brown Goode, this was, in fact, precisely the intent of Congress, to use the Smithsonian fund to support the museum of the United States. But Henry, by his aggressive refusal to consider such an assumption, forced a reconsideration of the idea by the abashed legislature. See G. Brown Goode, "The Genesis of the National Museum," *Annual Report for 1890–91,* 334.

frequently by Henry. In his *Annual Report for 1849* he echoed Silliman's fear, and added that "the tendency of an institution of this kind unless guarded against, will be to expend its funds on a heterogeneous collection of objects of mere curiosity."[62]

Henry felt that both museum and library should properly be "subservient to a living, active organization." The purpose of the museum operation would be "to collect only those [objects] which will yield a harvest of new results, and to preserve principally such as are not found in other collections, or will serve to illustrate and verify the Smithsonian publications."

The tendency of an Institution in which collections form a prominent object, is constantly towards a stationary condition: with a given income, the time must inevitably come when the expenditures necessary to accommodate the articles with house room and attendance will just equal the receipts. There is indeed no plan by which the funds of an Institution may be more inefficiently expended, than that of filling a costly building with an indiscriminate collection of objects of curiosity, and giving these in charge to a set of inactive curators.[63]

It is not to be assumed that Henry was unsympathetic or unconcerned about natural history. His interest was longstanding. In 1839 he attempted to ship a live alligator, procured by one of his Princeton students from Georgia, to Professor J. S. Henslow of Cambridge, England. Several attempts were made to send alligators, but all died before getting to the port of embarkation. Henry did manage to send to Henslow a less temperamental specimen of mica from Orange County, New York State.[64]

With the study of natural history, or any branch of knowledge now identified with museum collections,

---

[62] Silliman to Henry, Dec. 4, 1847, quoted in *Memorial of Joseph Henry*, 283; *Annual Report for 1849*, 20, s.v. "Museum."
[63] *Annual Report for 1850*, 8.
[64] Henry to Henslow, Dec. 2, 1839, Apr. 27, 1844, New-York Historical Society, New York.

Henry had no quarrel, so long as the purpose was the increase of knowledge and the dissemination of that increased knowledge throughout the world. In his *Annual Report for 1852* Henry wrote one of the most lyrical defenses of objects—properly used—ever penned:

Nothing in the whole system of nature is isolated or unimportant. The fall of a leaf and the motion of a planet are governed by the same laws. . . . It is in the study of objects, considered trivial and unworthy of notice by the casual observer, that genius finds the most important and interesting phenomena. It was in the investigation of the varying colors of the soap-bubble that Newton detected the remarkable fact of the fits of easy reflection and easy refraction presented by a ray of light in its passage through space, and upon which he established the fundamental principle of the present generalization of the undulatory theory of light. Smithson himself, the founder of this Institution, considered the analysis of a tear as nowise unworthy of his peculiar chemical skill.[65]

Similarly, in his *Annual Report for 1855*, Henry averred that "a life devoted exclusively to the study of a single insect, is not spent in vain. No animal however insignificant is isolated; it forms a part of the great system of nature, and is governed by the same general laws which control the most prominent beings of the organic world."[66]

Henry's attitude is most concisely expressed in his letter of December 14, 1876, to Mrs. Louis Agassiz, consoling her on the loss of her husband. "He found Natural History among us," wrote Henry "a mere method of forming discriptive catalogues of natural objects and left it a science of laws and causes."[67]

The cautious manner in which Henry appointed an assistant to take charge of the museum activities specified by Congress indicates his suspicious attitude to-

[65] P. 229.

[66] P. 20.

[67] SI Archives. The best biography of Agassiz is Edward Lurie, *Louis Agassiz, A Life in Science* (Chicago, 1960).

ward collections. Although numerous candidates offered themselves for the post besides Titian Ramsay Peale, Henry indicated his preference for a young naturalist from Dickinson College, Spencer F. Baird. Twenty-four years old when he applied for the position in 1847, Baird received a cool answer from Henry estimating that the Board of Regents would not appoint a curator until the building was in a proper condition to receive the specimens of natural history, a period which Henry estimated at not less than five years.[68]

Baird's eventual success in gaining the position was due to many factors. First of all was his promise as a naturalist and his competence in foreign languages.[69] Another factor was his friendship with George Perkins Marsh, representative from Vermont, and a member of the Board of Regents. Marsh was one among many who applied pressure to get the Smithsonian into the museum business at the earliest possible time. In a letter to Baird late in 1847, Marsh noted that "the Smithsonian Regents (before I became a member of the Board) had adopted a plan of operations which excluded all collections for some years, but I hope to break it up at the meeting next fall, if not before." It was Marsh's recommendation, moreover, which gave Baird the opportunity of translating and editing Brockhaus' *Bilder Atlas zum Conversations Lexicon,* a massive illustrated encyclopedia which a New York publisher, Charles Rudolph Garrigue, proposed to bring out in an English edition. By 1852, when the work was issued under the title of *The Iconographic Encyclopedia,* the widespread correspondence with American scientists which the new edition required had made Baird well known throughout the world of science in America.[70]

[68] Baird to Henry, Feb. 8 (?), 1847, and Henry to Baird, March 3, 1847, quoted in William Healey Dall, *Spencer Fullerton Baird, A Biography* (Philadelphia, 1915), 157, 163–64.

[69] Henry to his wife Harriet, July 19, 1850, SI Archives.

[70] Marsh to Baird, Dec. 30, 1847, quoted in Dall, *Baird,* 177; see also pp. 184–85.

More important, perhaps, was Baird's ability to relate his collecting activities to Henry's concern for the discovery of new truths. In a letter to Henry in the summer of 1849, following his application for employment, Baird asked "if it will be in accordance with your views for me to make an expedition, partly at the expense of the Smithsonian Institution, for the purpose of collecting specimens for its future museum. Professor Agassiz and I, when in Washington together, arranged a system of explorations, for the sake of more speedily and systematically getting a complete view of the ichthyology of our country." Henry advanced the necessary money for the purpose, $75.[71]

Henry's cautious support of exploratory expeditions under Smithsonian patronage did not affect his unwillingness to accept the already existing governmental collections of the Wilkes Expedition. As James Dwight Dana wrote in August 1849,

The fact is that Henry has no idea of requiring, yet a while, a curator. He intends to have nothing to do with the Exploring Expedition Collections or any other government property. I regret that he takes this stand,—for collections are better than books to the naturalist; they contain the whole that was ever put in words on the subject, and they illustrate a thousand times more. He is more interested in the library and publications,—both very important purposes,—but the plan is one sided—and not of the wide comprehensive character I had expected from Henry.[72]

Meanwhile, Baird was continuing to relate his exploration in natural history to Henry's general program for advancing knowledge. At the same time, Baird stated his respect and admiration for his future "boss" in naively effusive terms:

You must have been kept pretty busy this fall between your gigantic plans for the advancement of meteorological science, and the affairs of the Smithsonian In-

[71] Baird to Henry, June 9, 1849, Henry to Baird, June 13, 1849, *Ibid.*, 187–88.
[72] Dana to Baird, Aug. 27, 1849, *ibid.*, 189.

stitution Building. I think we are now in a fair way to have many knotty problems solved with regard to the mutual connection and causes of many natural phenomena. There certainly is no way in which the will of the founder of the Smithsonian Institution as to the increase of knowledge can be more effectively carried out than in taking charge of what no individual or even ordinary society could grasp. I consider the day as not very distant when many of the most interesting questions in natural and physical science shall be solved by the agencies set in motion by the institution, yourself at the head. How easy to call upon the trained meteorological correspondents for information upon other subjects, the distribution and local or general appearance of certain forms of animals, vegetables, or minerals; the occurrence of various diseases over the entire country; the spread and rate of progress of a pestilence as small pox, yellow fever, or cholera through the land; the range of action of noxious insects, as the Hessian fly, the cotton or tobacco worm, etc. with an infinity of others. I have long dreamed of some central association or influence which might call for such information, digest it, and then publish it in practical form to the world, and I see that my dream is not far from realization.

Baird looked forward with unabashed hope to the day when he could pursue his collecting activities in the name of the Smithsonian Institution "for making a true and genuine collection of objects of science."[73]

Perhaps even more important in Henry's eyes than the political and scientific recommendations Baird could muster was his youthful reverence for the distinguished scientist who was head of the Institution. The importance of a proper relationship between the Secretary and his assistants had probably been impressed upon Henry by his unfortunate experience with Jewett. Henry spelled out his definition of such a relationship in one of the last letters he wrote to Baird before recommending his appointment:

This being my view of the act of Congress, I shall protest against any interference with my preroga-

[73] Baird to Henry, Nov. 3, 1849, *ibid.*, 191, 193.

tives, and refuse to employ any person whom I think will not render me cordial assistance in carrying out the plans which I deem the best for the interests of the Institution. The assistants are responsible to the Secretary and the Secretary to the Regents; hence, all communications intended for the Regents or the Public must pass through his hands. These restrictions I am convinced are for the good of the whole and nothing would tend sooner to destroy the usefulness of the institution than the division of it into a number of separate interests. The whole establishment must be a unit and the effort of every one connected with it must be directed to the development of every part of the plan.

Henry left no doubt in Baird's mind about his concept of the role of the Museum. He regretted the necessity to spend $45,000 in addition to the original building estimate to fireproof the Library and Museum, but told Baird:

I fully agree in the propriety of the expenditure under the present circumstances, for if we are to have collections of a valuable character they should be deposited in a suitable building. The extra expenditure however will diminish the annual income of the Institution, and increase its natural tendency to assume a statical state, in which miscellaneous collections of objects of nature and art are merely exhibited as curiosities.[74]

By 1850, when the time came to appoint an assistant secretary to take charge of the Museum, Henry did not nominate his choice and request the Board to appoint him, as he had done in the case of Jewett, but "requested that he might be allowed to appoint an assistant in the department of natural history," which the Board authorized him to do, whereupon he "appointed Professor Spencer F. Baird under the foregoing resolution; and, on motion, the Board approved the appointment."[75] The different wording in the appointments of his two assistants is significant.

Henry was a strict administrator and his assistants

[74] April 23, 1850, *ibid.*, 208, 209.
[75] Rhees, ed., *Journals*, July 5, 1850, 67.

often felt the measure of his displeasure. In July 1852, he had informed Assistant Secretary Baird before the latter left on a trip to the West "that all the business must be in such a condition as to be at my command during his absence. The next day after his departure having occasion to write a letter to our agent in Paris I asked for the Foreign Correspondence. I was informed that this whole was locked up in the Prof's desk and the key not to be found. I directed B[aird] to be informed by letter that I should be obliged to break open his desk unless the key was forthcoming."[76]

The following year, in addition to expressing doubts about the quality of Baird's "Catalogue of North American Reptiles," the Secretary wrote to Bache, "I had a serious talk with Baird a few days ago just before he left for the West. He was as pliant and as affectionate as a young dog, but I fear he will sin again and nothing but a strong rein and a few hard knocks will keep him in the proper course."[77]

Although Baird appeared deferential and cooperative outwardly, he had purposes as distinct from Henry's as were the librarian Jewett's, and in the end he triumphed while the more unbending, self-righteous, and brilliant Jewett was fired. In an 1853 letter to his friend George P. Marsh, who was then in Constantinople, Baird revealed his own hopes for the future. After describing his efforts in equipping a number of exploring expeditions, he went on:

You ask who is to describe nondescripts, and what is to be done with the things when they come in. That is not my particular business now; my duty is to see that no chances are lost of advancing science, leaving the future to take care of itself. And indeed I expect the accumulation of a mass of matter thus collected (which the Institution cannot or will not "curate" efficiently) to have the effect of forcing our government into establishing a National Museum, of which (let me whis-

---

[76] Henry to Bache, July 16, 1852, SI Archives.
[77] July 11, 1853, *ibid.*

per it) *I* hope to be director. Still even if this argument don't weigh now; it will one of these days and I am content to wait.[78]

Henry's *Annual Report for 1850* laid down the guidelines for the Museum that were maintained until his acceptance of the U.S. government collections in 1857:

The act of Congress authorizing the establishment of the Smithsonian Institution, contemplates the formation of a Museum of Natural History. It would not, however, be in accordance with the spirit of the organization, to expend the income in the reproduction of collections of objects which are to be found in every museum of the country. Natural History can be much more effectually promoted, by special collections of new objects, by appropriations for original explorations and researches, and above all, by assistance in the preparation of the necessary drawings, and by presenting to the world, in a proper form, the labor of naturalists. In conformity with these views, it has been resolved to confine the collections principally, to objects of a special character, or to such as may lead to the discovery of new truths, or which may serve to verify or disprove existing or proposed scientific generalizations.

A separate appropriation for the upkeep of a large museum "would be equally objectionable," he wrote in his *Annual Report for 1849*, "since it would annually bring the institution before Congress as a supplicant for government patronage, and ultimately subject it to political influence and control."[79]

Henry's reluctance to receive the museum collections of the United States did not go unchallenged in Congress. On January 30, 1851, Senator Isaac P. Walker of Wisconsin introduced a resolution directing the Board of Regents of the Smithsonian to inform the Senate why suitable arrangements for the reception of "objects of art," natural history specimens, and the like

[78] July 2, 1853, quoted in Dall, *Baird*, 304–5.
[79] *Annual Report for 1850*, 21–22; *Annual Report for 1849*, 20–21.

had not been made in compliance with the sixth section of the Smithsonian Act. Jefferson Davis of Mississippi, one of the Regents, spoke out vigorously against the resolution. He insisted that while it was obligatory upon the government to deliver objects in its custody to the Smithsonian it was not obligatory upon the Smithsonian to receive them. He compared the proposed gift of the government museum to an elephant that might be given by the King of Siam to a minister whom he wished to crush. "The minister cannot refuse the present, because it comes from the King, but the expense of keeping the present crushes the minister. It is exactly such a present that the Senator from Wisconsin wishes to force the Smithsonian Institution to receive." Davis went so far as to accuse Senator Walker of attempting to "cripple" the Smithson fund "in the very object for which it was given." Davis said he took it for granted that the Smithsonian would "never want such a museum as that in the Patent Office"; still less did he think the Institution wished the plants brought back by the Wilkes expedition. "If they are not to be kept there," he concluded, "let the Government provide a room elsewhere, get rid of them, destroy them, or give them to somebody that will take them. But let not the Government coerce a fund, of which it was the chosen trustee, which was granted by a foreigner for a special purpose, with the charge of keeping this collection."[80]

Henry's conception of the purpose of the Museum was approved by the Special Congressional Committee set up in 1854 to examine the allocation of resources to the various projects of the Smithsonian. The committee reported:

The great object of the museum, should be to furnish to men of science, eminent in their several departments, the means of advancing knowledge in these departments, by submitting specimens of new objects to their examination. If the expenditure could be borne, it would scarcely be desirable to increase the number of

[80] Rhees, ed., *Documents* (1901), I, 471–77.

officers connected with the museum, so that the various branches of natural history might be fully represented; but considering the limited funds of the Smithsonian Institution, such an idea is not to be entertained.

The committee are satisfied, too, that the expenditures of the institution would be unprofitably increased by organizing it into several departments, with authority to the head of each department to expend the money appropriated to it. The tendency would be to more subdivisions of duty, to an increase of assistants, by the introduction first of temporary and then of permanent employés, until, as the collection grew larger and the persons charged with their care became more numerous, the greater portion of the income would be absorbed in salaries. Thus the munifience [sic] intended to increase and diffuse knowledge among mankind would be chiefly expended in salaries and official emoluments.[81]

But the support which the Special Congressional Committee gave Henry's views regarding the proper character of the Smithsonian's Museum was only a temporary victory, for in 1857 Henry was forced to accept the collections of the government. With this transfer went an appropriation of $4,000 annually, the same appropriation which had been granted to the United States Patent Office when it was in charge of the collection. As Henry predicted, the costs of caring for the collection rose more rapidly than the appropriation, and it was only by several years of supplication to Congress that the appropriation was raised to $10,000 in 1871, though still short of the actual expenses incurred. "So far from the Institution having derived advantage from the connection which has existed between it and the Museum," Henry noted in his *Annual Report for 1876*, "the latter has proved a serious obstacle in the way of the full development of the plan of the former in having absorbed, in the erection of the building and in the appropriations for the care of the specimens, at least one-half of the whole income of the

[81] Rhees, ed., *Journals*, 109, 111.

Smithson fund." Henry added in a ringing declaration that "every civilized government of the world has its museum which it supports with a liberality commensurate with its intelligence and financial ability, while there is but one *Smithsonian Institution*—that is, an establishment having expressly for its object 'the increase and diffusion of knowledge among men.' "[82]

Today it is sometimes assumed that only a great, rich, central museum can advance knowledge, while a small museum must be content with popular exhibits. Henry was no such pessimist. Every man, he felt, humble though he might be, could increase knowledge in some field or area—however small—if he would but put his mind and heart to it. When the Minnesota Academy of Natural Sciences was formed in 1873, Henry dispatched a congratulatory letter giving hints as to how its members could collect specimens, hold meetings, present papers, and publish proceedings.

What I have said relates to the uses of a local Academy of Sciences in the improvement of its members; but the importance of an establishment of this Kind should not be confined to the mere diffusion of Knowledge. It should endeavor to advance science by cooperating with other societies in the encouragement and institution of lines of original research. Thus it can make collections of the flora and fauna, of the fossils, rocks, minerals, etc., of a given region of which the location of the society is the centre and thereby contribute essentially to the general natural history of the continent.[83]

The intensity with which the venerable Secretary regarded this distinction between the increase and dif-

[82] *Annual Report for 1858*, 40, 56; Memorial to the Senate and House of Representatives, May 1, 1868, signed by S. P. Chase, Chancellor, and Joseph Henry, Secretary, printed in *Annual Report for 1867*, 114–15; *Annual Report for 1876*, 12–13. See also Goode, "The Genesis of the National Museum," 334–45; and "Discourse of W. B. Taylor," in *A Memorial of Joseph Henry*, 285.

[83] Henry to Alfred E. Ames, Corresponding Secretary of the Minnesota Academy of Natural Sciences, July 22, 1873, Minnesota Public Library, Minneapolis.

fusion of knowledge is evident in his letter of the following week to the Academy:

I write to apologize for the character of the letter addressed to the Secretary of the Minnesota Academy of Natural Sciences a few days ago. It was written before I had seen the copy of the Constitution of the Society from which I now learn that the establishment is intended exclusively for the advance of science and not as well for the intellectual improvement of the community among which it is founded, or, in other words, it is for the *increase* in contradistinction to the *diffusion* of Knowledge.

Henry went so far as to ask for the return of his first letter for which he promised a substitute "more in accordance with the objects of the Society."[84]

In his valedictory—his last annual report—Henry warned against merging the Smithsonian "in any establishment of the government" and pointed out the differing purposes of the Institution and the Museum:

The functions of the Institution and the Museum are entirely different; those of the Institution being—first, to enlarge the bounds of human thought by assisting men of science to make original investigations in all branches of knowledge, to publish these at the expense of the Smithson fund, and to present copies of them to all the principal libraries of the world; second, to institute investigations in various branches of science and explorations for the collection of specimens in natural history and ethnology to be distributed to museums and other establishments; third, to diffuse knowledge by carrying on an extended international series of exchanges by which the accounts of all the original researches in science, the educational progress, and the general advance of civilization in the New World are exchanged for similar works of the Old World. To carry out this plan the Institution requires no costly building, but merely accommodations for receiving and distributing its collections.

The Museum, on the other hand, is intended to embrace a collection of specimens of nature and art which

[84] July 30, 1873, *ibid.* See also Martha C. Bray, "The Minnesota Academy of Natural Sciences," *Minnesota History*, XXXIX (1964), 111–22. I am indebted to Mrs. Bray for these references.

shall exhibit the natural resources and industries of the country, or to present at one view the materials essential to the condition of high civilization which exists in the different States of the American Union; to show the various processes of manufacture which have been adopted by us, as well as those used in foreign countries; in short, to form a great educational establishment by means of which the inhabitants of our own country, as well as those of foreign lands who visit our shores, may be informed as to the means which exist in the United States for the enjoyment of human life in the present, and the improvement of these means in the future.

The support of such an establishment must, of necessity, be derived from Congress and no part of the income of the Smithson fund should be devoted to this purpose, since it is evident from the will of Smithson that he intended his benefaction for the good of mankind, and therefore all expenditures on local objects, or even on those limited to the United States, are not in conformity with the intentions of the donor.[85]

In his private correspondence, Henry was even more concerned with the relationship between the Museum and the Smithsonian. The problem had been brought to a head by the great Philadelphia Centennial celebration in 1876 and the enormous haul of objects given to the National Museum by the foreign and domestic exhibitors following the exhibition. "The result of the Centennial," wrote Henry, "has produced, as I predicted in my last report, a crisis in the history of the Smithsonian Institution." A new building was "absolutely necessary" to accommodate the objects which amounted "in bulk [to] four times the space of the present Smithsonian edifice." "The Museum is destined to become a very large establishment, commanding considerable patronage and is at all times liable to be brought under direct political influence: the association while advantageous to the Museum is dangerous to the future of the Institution."[86]

Henry wrote to another friend:

[85] *Annual Report for 1877*, 8.
[86] Henry to B. A. Gould, Jan. 30, 1877, SI Archives.

The only remaining object that stands in the way of carrying out my original idea is the Museum, and as an approximation toward being relieved of this, we have received within the last 3 years $20,000 annually for its care and maintainance, beside a very liberal appropriation for making a display at the Centennial. . . .

But now comes the danger. The appropriations of Congress for the Museum are fitful and can only be obtained in the name of the Smithsonian Institution by a process to which I am not fitted, that of lobbying. If the appropriation fail in any year, the expense of maintaining the Museum must fall upon the Institution.

Furthermore the process of lobbying can only be carried on by rewarding—directly or indirectly—the lobbyist.

The Institution in this way is liable to fall under political dominium, and, finally, be presided over by some distinguished politician.

It is, therefore, my serious conviction that for the safe administration of the Smithson fund in the future, it ought to be entirely separated from what we have denominated a "National Museum."

Unfortunately there are some Members of the Board of Regents, who strenuously oppose this proposition and think the popularity of the Establishment would be damaged by such a separation.

They do not fully apprehend the fact that the Institution is not a popular establishment depending on popular reputation for its support, but the establishment of an individual for scientific purposes, and supplied with sufficient funds to carry on its own operations without any appeal to Congress.

The proposition which I desire to carry out, but which I see great difficulty in accomplishing is, that the Government purchase the Smithsonian building say for $300,000, or a little more than one half of its actual cost; that $200,000 of this be added to the principal and $100,000 be devoted to the erection of a building containing necessary compartments for the storage of exchanges and offices, a chemical, biological and a physical laboratory.[87]

Henry's death in 1878, so soon after the problem brought on by the Centennial, spelled failure to his

[87] Henry to J. P. Lesley, Jan. 12, 1877, *ibid.*

concept of the proper relationship between the National Museum and the Smithsonian. His one remaining task—to separate the United States National Museum from the Smithsonian—was never accomplished. The patient, pliant Baird waited, and was rewarded, not only with the National Museum but with the Smithsonian Institution itself. On Henry's death Baird was appointed Secretary. As was to be expected, the new Secretary rushed to completion what Henry had sought to prevent.

The change of policy, the undoing of Henry's program of "active operations," foreseen by Henry in his *Annual Report for 1852,* had begun. It was not a radical turnabout, and whether it had the effect that Henry foresaw of "paralyz[ing] the spirit of activity" must be judged by historians of the various fields of scholarly endeavor in which the Smithsonian has been engaged. One historian of science has written that from 1857, when Henry accepted custody of the government collections, "the history of the Smithsonian Institution can be described as a frittering away of Henry's conception and the conversion of the Institution to a museum. The remaining activities in research became largely overshadowed by the care of the contents of what was to become aptly described as the nation's attic."[88]

While this judgment is exaggerated and neglects the strong contribution made by scientists in the Natural History Museum, it nevertheless expresses an attitude common among laymen and scholars alike. It also reflects a value judgment made in Henry's time and at the present time concerning the significance of two types of "original research." One type involves the careful accumulation of large collections of specimens

---

[88] *Annual Report for 1852,* 225. Nathan Reingold, ed., *Science in Nineteenth-Century America: A Documentary History* (New York, 1964), 153; for a similar assessment, see D. S. Greenberg's account of the Smithsonian in *Science,* CXLVII (March 12, 1965), 1266–69.

16. Preparing models for exhibition, *ca.* 1890.

17. Ethnology Laboratory, Smithsonian Institution, *ca.* 1890.

in various fields of human inquiry, their detailed description, and their classification into a system of organization. Such descriptive, taxonomic, systematic investigations comprise Baird's personal scholarly contribution to knowledge. He published numerous and significant studies of this sort, particularly in mammalogy, ichthyology, and ornithology, which became reference points and building blocks for further work in those fields. As two appreciative commentators have put it:

Baird was not a theorist and did not worry much over the origin of forms; much of his work in fact antedated Darwin's illuminations. He described what he saw, and in such fashion that no subsequent observer had any doubt as to what he meant. This persistence in accuracy is the foundation of the "Baird School" in ornithology, so ably represented by Elliott Coues, Joel A. Allen, Robert Ridgway, John Cassin, Thomas M. Brewer, and the American ornithologists of today.[89]

The other type of "original research" involves the imaginative formulation and testing of hypotheses, integrative conceptualizations, and explanatory laws. Such investigations, particularly in electricity, electromagnetism, and acoustics, comprise Henry's personal scholarly contribution to knowledge. The first type of research is primarily identified with the collection and preservation of museum collections; the latter with laboratory experimentation sometimes involving utilization of museum objects, but not primarily concerned with their preservation. Those engaged in research of the second sort sometimes disparage research of the first type. Scholars engaged in taxonomic work, on the other hand, acidly point out that the theorists

[89] See David Starr Jordan and Jessie Knight Jordan in *DAB*, s.v. "Baird, Spencer Fullerton." For Baird's bibliography, see George Brown Goode, *The Published Writings of Spencer Fullerton Baird, 1843–1882* in United States National Museum, *Bulletin No. 20* (Washington, D.C., 1883), iii–xvi, 1–377. For a general account of the work of Baird and his followers, see Remington Kellogg, "A Century of Progress in Smithsonian Biology," *Science*, CIV (August 9, 1946), 132–41.

must rely upon the objective record patiently built up by the taxonomist and note that the significance of theories often takes on an academic, or historical, interest, after the passage of time, while the objects retain their documentary uniqueness.

Because Henry feared that the Smithsonian would become primarily identified with the activities of its museum, of which Baird was the principal exponent, he fought to separate the Smithsonian from its embrace. While he supported the advance of knowledge in natural history, as well as in other fields of human inquiry, he profoundly feared for the future of the Smithsonian Institution if it became museum-oriented rather than research-oriented. He did not, of course, mean to imply that the two aims were mutually exclusive. But he did theorize that excessive concern with museum requirements would seriously impair the ability of the Institution to "increase knowledge."

Henry's fears were carefully explained in a letter to Professor Louis Agassiz in 1865: "The collection and distribution of new materials for the advance of Natural History is an important object of the special mission of the Smithsonian Institution while the description and preservation of specimens does not in my opinion, form an essential part of the general plan of the establishment and should be devolved on other parties who are willing and able to discharge the duty." Henry went on to note that

the existence of the Smithsonian show museum is due simply to the fact that the Government made the Institution the curator of its specimens. Had the [Wilkes] exploring expedition never been undertaken, the Institution would not have been obliged to expend more than 30 thousand dollars instead of 235 thousand on a building. The mere excess of the interest of the latter over that of the former sum would keep in the field a large number of explorers, who would collect sufficient specimens, in a few years, to supply all the museums of the world with full illustrations of the products of the American continent. But it is not alone of the original cost of the building I have to complain, but also of the great expense of keeping it in repair and the constant and natural tendency to absorb, in the increase of the specimens, an undue portion of the income. From the experience I have had of the great cost of moving, arranging, and preserving the specimens, even those of mineralogy, I am more and more convinced of the necessity of restricting the number of statistical objects and the importance of distributing the duplicate specimens as rapidly as may be for the increase and diffusion of knowledge among men.

Since, however, we are at least, for the present, obliged to support a museum, we should study to render it, as far as possible, subservient to the general policy of the Institution, by making such collections, as are not usually found in the museums of this country and can be preserved with comparatively small expense. With this view, I am much in favour of collecting all the specimens of Ethnology which can be procured, to illustrate the antiquities of this continent.[90]

Henry's fears were shared by Agassiz. In one of his letters to the Smithsonian Secretary in 1867, the founder of Harvard's Museum of Comparative Zoology noted that "I am crushed by the Museum and see no chance of relief. . . . The more I see what a Museum requires to be successful, the more am I satisfied that the Smiths[sonian] ought not to spread its resources to build up a Museum, unless Congress provides ample means for that specific purpose."[91]

In Henry's scale of values, taxonomic research counted for little in comparison with theoretical research. Baird was useful to him because someone had to run the ever-growing museum, and Baird was an efficient administrator who organized and coordinated many of the exploring activities that sent specimens pouring back to the Smithsonian.

Henry saw the uniqueness of the Smithsonian Insti-

[90] June 10, 1865, Mary Henry's typescript copy of missing original draft or letter of her father, SI Archives. Additional punctuation, which was probably supplied by Miss Henry, has been removed and certain apparent typing errors silently corrected.

[91] Agassiz to Henry, April 15, 1867, *ibid.*

tution increasingly threatened by the growth of the
United States National Museum. Others, like Agassiz,
worried that Baird, as head of that museum, would
abandon or sabotage Henry's policy of making museum
operations subservient to the central purpose of the
Smithsonian. The head—or potential head—of an institution dedicated to the advancement of knowledge
must be an unquestioned leader in advancing knowledge, as Henry was. Baird's qualifications were unsat-
isfactory to those who rated theoretical research
above descriptive research. The issue came to a head at
the meeting of the newly organized National Academy
of Sciences in New Haven in 1864, where Agassiz led a
desperate fight to prevent the election of Baird to the
Academy on the grounds that he had made no original
contribution to knowledge. Agassiz's fight against
Baird was complicated by professional and personal
disagreements. Among these points of issue was Agassiz's proposal, at the March 15, 1864, meeting of the
Board of Regents of the Smithsonian, to increase the
efficiency of the "active operations" of the Institution
by relieving it of the burden of maintaining a museum,
a library, and a gallery of art.[92]

Though Henry supported Baird's election to the
Academy, it is clear that he did so not because he
disagreed with Agassiz about the significance of
Baird's research, but for practical reasons. In his letter
of August 13, 1864, to Agassiz, Henry discussed his
reasons at length, commencing with his critique of the
unusually rapid and secret formation of the National
Academy of Sciences:

My anticipations in several particulars have been realized—an antagonism, such as I feared, has been produced in the minds of those who think themselves ill
used in being left out; while a considerable number of
those who were elected feel that they ought to have
been consulted in making out the list of names. The
feeling also exists, to a considerable extent, that the

[92] Rhees, ed., *Journals*, 221–22.

few who organized the academy intend to govern it; and I think this was the *animus* which excited the determination to elect Professor Baird. He was the choice of a large majority of the cultivators of Natural History; and although your opposition was honest in intention, and your position correct in general principle yet I think that had you prevailed in your opposition, a majority of all the naturalists would have resigned; and a condition of affairs would have been produced deeply to be deplored. I fully agree with you in opinion, and I presume the philosophical world would also concur with you, that as a class of investigations those which relate to Physiology and the mode of production and existence of organic forms are of a higher order than those which belong to descriptive Natural History. The good however, which two persons may have done to science in these two classes will depend on the relative amount, as well as, on the character of their labours. Besides this you ought to have commenced with the application of principle of the higher investigations, in the formation of the Academy, for you could not reasonably expect that any member would vote to disparage his own pursuit.

It is true I voted for Mr. Baird and taking all things into consideration I am sure I did right in doing so. I do not agree with you in thinking that my having voted for him will give him power to control the policy of the Institution; neither do I think that the proposition you made at the meeting of the Board of Regents has any connection whatever with the vote in the academy. It is the same which I have advocated from the first, and which I doubt not will meet the approval of the majority of the intelligent naturalists of the world. If Mr. Baird should attempt to interfere with the policy of the Institution I would not hesitate to ask him to resign, and to insist on his doing so; as I did in the case of Mr. Jewett. But I have not the least idea of any trouble with him in this way; or that for many years to come anything can be done in the way of carrying out your proposition.[93]

[93] Benjamin Peirce Papers, Harvard University Archives, Cambridge, Mass., printed as appendix to A. Hunter Dupree, "The Founding of the National Academy of Sciences—A Reinterpretation," American Philosophical Society, *Proceedings*, CI (1957), 438–40. See also Lurie, *Agassiz*, 343; A. Hunter Dupree, *Asa Gray, 1810–1888* (Cambridge, Mass., 1959), 322.

Two days later Henry wrote to Professor Bache about the meeting and noted that

our friends, from Cambridge, were much displeased because they did not succeed in preventing the election of Professor Baird. They were right in principle, but wrong in practice. I fully agree with Agassiz that physiological researches is a higher order of scientific investigation than the description of species but the *amount*, of labour as well as the *kind*, must be taken into consideration and as all the naturalists with the exception of Agassiz and one or two others have made their reputation and were elected into the Academy on account of just such work as Baird has done the opposition of Agassiz who stood alone was considered against the whole class and had he succeeded in keeping Baird out by urging a rule of the Academy, the majority of naturalists would have withdrawn.

It will not do to press a principle, in some cases too far. In this democratic country we cannot expect in all instances to carry out points and must be content in doing what we can instead of what we would.[94]

Baird was elected to the Academy and, on Henry's death, succeeded him as Secretary of the Institution. Baird never challenged Henry's policy when he was alive; rather, he outlived Henry and his policy. The symbol of the shift in emphasis from Henry's analytic genius to Baird's descriptive gifts, from Henry's definition of original research to Baird's, was the galvanic reversal in the relationship between the Museum and the Institution, from repulsion to attraction, from Henry to Baird.

Publication

Henry's belief in the importance of publication was laid down flatly in his "Programme of Organization": "Knowledge can be increased by different methods of facilitating and promoting the discovery of new truths; and can be most extensively diffused among men by means of the press."[95] Having personally suf-

[94] Aug. 15, 1864, SI Archives.

[95] Henry's "Programme of Organization" as printed in any of his *Annual Reports*.

fered in his reputation by failure to publish—in timely fashion—the results of some of his scientific investigations, Henry was peculiarly sensitive to the importance of the press. That he accepted the significance of the publication function of the Smithsonian is also demonstrated by the detailed editorial work that he himself undertook from the very beginning. His correspondence is replete with references to this function. It is particularly evident in his extended correspondence with E. G. Squier, whose *American Archaeological Researches: An Inquiry into the Origin and Purposes of the Aboriginal Monuments and Remains of the Mississippi Valley,* with E. H. Davis, was the first of the Smithsonian's Contributions to Knowledge series. Henry insisted upon throwing out some of the engravings Squier had prepared which were not "of an original character," and he drew a tight line on the manuscript itself so that "your first labours should be given to the world as free as possible from every thing of a speculative nature and that your positive addition to the sum of human knowledge should stand in bold relief unmingled with the labours of others." As John Russell Bartlett put it, "In due time the work was printed and proved to be the most valuable contribution, by far, that had yet been made to American Archaeology."[96]

The frugal Henry did not waste precious Smithsonian funds on publications that failed to advance knowledge. Annual Reports of the Institution were customarily printed by Congress at public expense. When Jefferson Davis of Mississippi was asked by a fellow senator, following a motion to order the printing of the Smithsonian Annual Report for 1850, why the Smithsonian did not print its own proceedings, he replied: "The Smithsonian Institution does print its contributions to knowledge, and does attend to their diffu-

[96] Henry to Squier and Davis, Feb. 16, 1848, Squier Papers, Manuscript Division, Library of Congress; Bartlett's MS Autobiography, p. 42, in John Carter Brown Library, Providence, R.I.

sion among men. This, however, is not a contribution to
human knowledge, but is a report to Congress of the
manner in which the Board of Regents executed the
trust confided to them."[97] The Report was ordered to be
printed.

In correspondence with friends Henry could joke
about the problems he had to overcome in convincing
Congress and the public about the value of some of the
Smithsonian's publishing activities. Writing to Samuel
F. Haven, librarian of the American Antiquarian Society in 1859, Henry commented that the Institution
was "growing in reputation and usefulness notwithstanding the abuse we occasionally receive for expend-
ing the income of the bequest in publishing such useless
trash as grammars of Indian and negro languages."[98]
With his ironic letter, Henry enclosed a copy of the
recently published Smithsonian study of the Yoruba
language.

When it is realized that the original act of Congress
creating the Smithsonian Institution made no mention
of publishing activities, a fact occasionally brought out
by Henry's opponents, the criticism engendered by the
Secretary's willingness to publish at all, let along a
Yoruba grammar, can well be imagined.

Henry constantly drew a distinction between the
"active operations of the Institution" and those which
he considered static. Included in his definition of active
operations for the year 1852 were the published results
of explorations in the Southwest; the publication of
original papers on physiology, comparative anatomy,
zoology, and natural history; the furnishing of instruments to various exploring expeditions for the study
of terrestrial magnetism, and the publication of the
results; the collection and publication of statistics of
the libraries of the United States and the perfection of
a plan for stereotyping library catalogues; the awaken-

[97] Rhees, ed., *Documents* (1901), March 7, 1851, I, 479–80.
[98] April 27, 1859, American Antiquarian Society Archives,
Worcester, Mass.

18. Preparing models for exhibition, *ca.* 1890.

19. Exhibit Hall—Comparative Anatomy, Smithsonian Institution, *ca.* 1890

ing of attention of scholars to American Indian archeology, ethnology, and linguistics; and the establishment of a system of international literary and scientific exchange of scholarly publications.[99] The unifying feature of all these active operations was the publication of newly discovered knowledge. The knowledge might emerge from what we would now call museum operations, library operations, and administrative operations. Henry had no prejudice concerning their source. His sole criterion was that they must advance knowledge. In the stirring formative years of the Smithsonian, almost everything did.

Henry, indeed, could conceive of the government of the United States being dissolved, but not the "Smithsonian Contributions to Knowledge" which, in such an eventuality, would "still be found in the principal libraries of the world, a perpetual monument of the wisdom and liberality of the founder of the Institution, and of the faithfulness of those who first directed its affairs."[100]

Education

Education—usually in the form of universities or normal schools—was the almost universal recommendation of those in the period 1836–46 who considered how the Smithson bequest should be applied. Yet the educational function was not incorporated in the provisions of the act establishing the Smithsonian Institution. There is only one reason for this omission: John Quincy Adams. Adams successfully fought, blocked, and argued against all proposals to create educational institutions, which he pointed out were designed to disseminate existing knowledge, not to create new knowledge. Despite Adams' success in this legislative fight, Henry was forced to meet the continuing public

[99] *Annual Report for 1852,* 224–25.
[100] *Ibid.,* 226.

assumption that education was the principal purpose of the Smithsonian. The new Secretary minced no words in attacking the concept. As he bluntly stated: "The objects of the Smithsonian Institution are not educational. The press in our country already teems with elementary works on the different branches of knowledge, and to expend our funds in adding to these, would be to dissipate them without perceptible effect. Neither do we believe that the distribution of penny magazines, or tracts on the rudiments of science, can ever supersede the labors of the school master."[101]

In his *Report for 1853* Henry was still battling the common misapprehension:

Nothing apparently can be further from the truth than the idea which was first prevalent in this country that Smithson left his money merely to diffuse practical knowledge among the people of the United States. On the contrary he intended this institution as a monument to his name which should be known to all men, and prized by the student of every branch of literature and science, which should not be restricted to merely spreading abroad the knowledge which already exists, but, above all, should be the means of enlarging the bounds of human thought.[102]

The reversal in the image of the Smithsonian in later years is paralleled by the changed image of the university. In the mid-nineteenth century, as James B. Conant has pointed out, "the colleges viewed their professors primarily as teachers rather than as research men." Joseph Henry put it more pungently:

We have in the United States upwards of a hundred colleges each one of which has a corps of Professors in the line of science and yet scarcely any one of them makes an attempt to enlarge the bounds of human knowledge. The truth is we are over-run in this country with charlatanism; our newspapers are filled with

[101] Adams, *The Great Design,* ed. Washburn; *Annual Report for 1848,* 33.
[102] p. 7–8.

the puffs of quackery and every man who can burn phosphorous in oxygen and exhibit a few experiments to a class of young Ladies is called a man of Science.[103]

The Smithsonian, established in the face of the prevailing unconcern for research, encouraged and supported those who were advancing knowledge while vigorously eschewing the instructional chores that formed the principal purpose of the educational institutions of the country. Now, of course, any self-respecting university considers itself primarily a center for advancing knowledge. Research has been elevated to a primary role; teaching—as such—is honored verbally, but not practically. While this evolution has occurred in the universities, the Smithsonian has become identified more and more with the teaching—through exhibits—of established knowledge. Scholars—particularly in fields in which the Smithsonian has not distinguished itself in the past—are often unaware that it has any function other than popular education.

Henry not only eschewed educational tasks as a function of Smithsonian, but enjoined research responsibilities upon the universities. In discussing with his friend Bache the filling of an important academic chair in 1852, he asserted:

All things being equal the one ought to be preferred [to an important university chair] who has evinced the greatest talent and industry in the way of original research. I do not for an instant subscribe to the proposition advanced by Olmstead[,] Frazer, and others that the most original man is the worst teacher—that he will be constantly talking about his own researches rather than imparting a knowledge of the general principles of the science. There is always an enthusiasm in an original investigator and a breadth of thought which awakes in a class a spirit which a second hand teacher can never arouse. Take for example as the two

[103] Conant, "The Advancement of Knowledge in the United States in the Nineteenth Century," *Colorado Quarterly*, XI (1963), 234; draft of letter from Henry to "My dear Sir," July 27, 1846, SI Archives.

extremes of the two classes a Faraday as the positive pole and a Webster of Cambridge as the negative then fill up the intermediate ordinates with less striking examples and we shall have a preponderance of instances in favor of the original investigator. Besides this nothing can make up in the pride of a class in the reputation of their teacher for his want of originality as an author. Have you ever seen a pamphlet on this subject by Professor Olmstead? It is a plea for stupidity or an apology for dunces. I think if I can find a copy I shall notice it in a communication I have promised to the Educational Association which meets at New-ark. An opinion of this kind if adopted would prove in the highest degree prejudicial to the advance of true knowledge in our country.[104]

Henry never ceased to demand the fullest exploitation of the research possibilities already existent in established academic chairs. There is a note of irritation in his letter to President Thomas Hill of Harvard recommending Professor Wolcott Gibbs of New York for the vacant Rumford Professorship in 1863. Henry wrote:

The only reward which our country offers to one who devotes his life to original research in any branch of science, is the election to a chair in one of our higher institutions of learning, and, in my opinion, other qualifications being equal, the appointment ought to be given to the candidate who has contributed most to the advance of the branch of science pertaining to the chair to be filled. I cannot, for a moment, subscribe to the proposition announced by a professor in one of the colleges of New England, that a man who has actually extended the bounds of knowledge by original research is, on that account, as a general rule less qualified to teach than one who has merely made himself acquainted with what others have done. On the contrary I am convinced by my own observations that the successful investigator possesses talents and enthusiasm which scarcely ever fails, by awakening sympathy and exciting admiration, to make an impression on the student which will influence his future life.[105]

[104] Henry to Bache, June 25, 1852, *ibid.*
[105] Feb. 16, 1863, Harvard University Archives. Henry's attitude on this subject was frequently expressed. See, for example,

It might be well to consider the influence the Smithsonian, under Joseph Henry's leadership, had on encouraging the development of basic research in the universities. By providing positive support to scholarly activity at a time when the universities were largely uninterested, Henry may have provided an all-important example and alternative which forced the more rapid evolution of this trend in the somnolent centers of undergraduate instruction.

Summation

In the great controversy brought on by Henry's firing of Jewett, the attacks on Henry's concept of the purpose of the Smithsonian swelled to a chorus. During the congressional investigation that followed, the position of the anti-Henry forces was stated most forcefully by Representative Upham, who asserted:

The word 'INCREASE' is held by some of the zealous combatants in the Smithsonian controversy to be identical with 'DISCOVERY.' The idea seems to be that knowledge can only be *increased* by the *discovery of new truth*. This is an arbitrary and untenable position. A mind experiences an increase of knowledge if it knows more than it did before, although all the ideas it has received may be in the commonest text-books. There has been an increase of knowledge in the school, in the congregation, in the lecture-room, if ideas not before known to them have been received into the minds of the hearers; even, indeed, it matters not if those ideas have been recorded for thousands of years in languages, classical or sacred, that have been dead long ago. Knowledge has been increased if one mind has received more, whether it be new or old truth. The language of Smithson is perfectly simple, and in its natural sense covers the whole ground; it includes, but does not require *new* truth. Truth discovered a thousand years ago is as good as truth discovered yesterday. Knowl-

draft of his letter of Aug. 13, 1846, to "My dear Sir," SI Archives.

edge embraces it all alike, and Smithson's object was to carry knowledge where it was not before, and to increase it where it was; to spread it over a wide area and to a greater depth.[106]

The philosophy behind Upham's conception expired (at least temporarily) with the defeat of the attempt to censure Henry in 1855 for his dismissal of Jewett. Henry emerged triumphant, and in the succeeding years few were able to challenge his interpretation of the meaning of Smithson's will, which he continued aggressively to impress upon thinkers throughout the country.

One of the finest statements of Henry's conception of the purpose of the Smithsonian is, appropriately enough, located in the Massachusetts Historical Society, whose dedication to the ideal of supporting the advance of knowledge is supreme among historical societies. In an 1867 letter to the historian George Bancroft, then serving as U.S. Minister to Prussia, Henry put it this way:

You may recollect that, from the first, my idea has been that the whole income, derived from the Smithsonian fund, should be appropriated to the advancement of abstract science. I adopted this view because I am sure that it is in strict accordance with the will of the founder and best adapted to advance the cause of humanity. . . .

It is, therefore, evident that if we would advance to a higher civilization some of the elements, at least, of this more elevated condition must be found in the progress of science. In regard to this there are three considerations; 1st, the *discovery* of the laws of nature, which constitute science; 2d, the *diffusion* of the knowledge of these laws, which comprises a portion of education, and, 3d, their *application* to the wants of life. Now it is evident that the second and third considerations depend upon the first. It is true that we may continue to teach the same principles to generation after generation, and to apply the same laws to the same, or similar, inventions but in this there is but little progress.

[106] *Upham Report*, p. 15.

With these views, it has appeared to me remarkable that so little provision is made in civilized countries for the advancement of abstract science. The appropriations of Government and the benevolent bequests of individuals are, almost exclusively, confined to education, while the most trivial application of a scientific principle is frequently rewarded with that which would serve to support a whole class of savans, it may be, of the French Institute.

I have been assiduously labouring for the last 20 years to enforce these propositions, through the means of the Smithsonian Institution, and to prove that the true province of this establishment is neither to diffuse nor apply science, but, primarily to increase it, and this by the application of all the funds unencumbered to the facilitating of research in the various branches of human thought.

Museums, Libraries and galleries of art are local Establishments and ought to be provided for, directly, by the Government, or by the people among whom they are located; but funds appropriated expressly for the increase of knowledge ought not to be expended upon these objects, however important they may be in themselves.

These ideas were, however, too much in advance of the intelligence of our country at the time of incorporation of the Institution, and, hence the large expenditures that were made on the building and other local objects. We have made, however, during the past year an important advance towards the realization of these conceptions, by the transfer of our Library, for safe keeping and support, to the care of Congress. By this arrangement, though we still retain the use of our books, in addition to those of the Library of Congress, we save nearly *ten* thousand dollars annually in binding, cataloguing, attendance &c. . . .

There remains one step further to be taken in regard to the Institution and that is, the establishment, by the Government, of a museum, or a collection of objects of nature and art, and in which the specimens which have already been collected by the Institution, as well as those belonging to the Government, might be deposited.[107]

[107] Nov. 21, 1867, Massachusetts Historical Society, Boston, Mass. For a similar statement, see Henry's *Annual Report for 1859.*

In a letter to the English scholar John Tyndall in 1872, Henry reiterated his lifelong mission:

It is only after nearly twenty-five years of struggle and entire devotion to this Institution that I have begun to make the country appreciate the difference between the discovery of new truths, and the teaching of old ones; to make apparent the three relations of knowledge, namely, (1) The discovery of new truths; (2) the teaching of scientific principles; and (3) the application of scientific principles to useful purposes in the arts. The 2nd and 3rd of these relations have almost exclusively been recognized and provision made for their advancement. There are however many wealthy individuals in this country who may be induced to found establishments for investigations either in connection with our older educational Institutions or on a separate basis.[108]

Henry had constantly to fight against those who equated success with popularity. When a member of Congress once told Henry that by a few changes in his policies involving only a moderate reduction of the income of the Institution, great praise might be won from the press, and the Smithsonian made a "popular" establishment, Henry assured his kindly intentioned friend that "his self-imposed mission and deliberate purpose was to prevent, as far as in him lay, precisely that consummation."[109]

In his *Annual Report for 1876,* Henry took up the question of Smithsonian popularity:

It has been supposed that the Institution has derived much benefit from its connection with the Museum in the way of adding to its popularity, but it should be recollected that the Institution is not a popular establishment and that it does not depend for its support upon public patronage, but that it is an establishment founded on the bequest of an *individual,* and that the

[108] Oct. 22, 1872, Rhees Papers, Henry E. Huntington Library and Art Gallery, San Marino, Calif.

[109] "Discourse of W. B. Taylor," in *Memorial of Joseph Henry,* 282–83n.

very nature of its operations, involving study and investigation, is in a considerable degree incompatible with continued interruption from large numbers of visitors.

"Opinions," Henry noted in his *Report for 1853,* "ought to be weighed rather than counted."[110]

The relationship between the maintenance of collections of objects and the advancement of knowledge is difficult to assess in all its implications. Nevertheless, it seems fair to say that Henry foresaw the dangers of intellectual sterility that can be induced by the responsibility for the collection and care of objects when that activity is not subservient to an overriding commitment to the advancement of knowledge.

Henry's single-minded devotion to his conception of the purpose of the Smithsonian reminds one of a military man's dedication to the conception of the military "mission." Under the concept of the "mission" a responsible commander must organize his resources to accomplish a briefly defined goal set by higher authority. The apparent simplicity of the task is belied by historical examples too numerous to list of generals who allowed their view of the mission to be clouded by subsidiary considerations. The ease of forgetting the mission of a military force in peacetime is particularly acute and particularly fatal. Frequently the weight of physical installations, material comfort, and nonessential organization structures cause the peacetime military commander to forget that his only purpose is success in combat. Henry resolved that no one would forget the mission of the Smithsonian. His public reports, his public and private interviews with members of Congress and others, his private correspondence, all reiterate the supreme importance of remembering the mission.

In his *Report for the Year 1850* Henry emphasized the necessity of republishing the terms of the Smithson

[110] *Annual Report for 1876,* 12; *Annual Report for 1853,* 7.

bequest, and also the general principles of the plan adopted to carry it out, in order to let the public know what the Institution was accomplishing, and also what ought to be expected from it. "There is a tendency in the management of public institutions," Henry went on, "to lose sight of the object for which they were established, and hence it becomes important frequently to advert to the principles by which they ought to be governed."[111]

Henry allowed nothing to deflect him from the pursuit of his mission. Even members of Congress were directly attacked when they tried to distort the true purpose of Smithson's bequest. An amusing instance of this inflexible purpose was demonstrated by Henry during the course of a meeting of an Agricultural Convention in the Smithsonian lecture room in 1852. Henry happened to enter as the members, led by Senator Stephen A. Douglas of Illinois, were discussing the means by which the Smithsonian Institution might be converted into an organization to aid the agriculturists of the country. The matter, Henry had learned, had previously been discussed by a committee of Congress, and some had proposed that Henry be called in to give his opinion of the project. To this, Henry reported, "Douglas objected stating that he knew that I would object to anything but the publication of sea weeds and such trash." Henry entered the hall just as Douglas began speaking and "immediately put myself in a position to catch the eye of the President and to be heard and seen from every part of the room." Henry, when allowed to speak, then stated hotly

that the money was not given to the United States exclusively for its own benefit but for the good of man—given in trust for a special object, and that it would be an everlasting disgrace to our country if the trustees of this fund should divert it from its proper object and devote it to their own use &c. I was very much excited and I fear was rather severe in my re-

[111] p. 6.

marks. The whole however passed off very well and Judge D. found he had made a mistake.[112]

Henry and Douglas got together the next day and harmonized their views. Needless to say, to effect that harmony Henry forced Douglas to move to his point of view.

In his Anniversary Address as President of the Philosophical Society of Washington, November 18, 1871, Henry pointed out the simple purpose of a society devoted to the advancement of knowledge. "The bane of many societies," he noted, "is the time consumed in details of business and in the discussion of non-essential points relative to their government. . . . For the government of men whose object is the advance of *truth*, but few rules are necessary, and these, unlike the laws of the Medes and Persians—expressed in inexorable codes—must consist of simple principles, readily adaptable to all contingencies."[113]

Henry's interpretation of the will of Smithson required that all the activities of the Smithsonian Institution be subordinated to one idea: the increase of knowledge, and its subsequent diffusion. This was the mission that Henry preached to one and all with a religious fervor. This was the idea that governed his administration of the Smithsonian's congressionally endowed activities: museum, library, and lectures. The Smithsonian had a sense of purpose under Henry. In the practical and materialistic world of mid-nineteenth-century America, Henry raised the banner of theoretical research and the ideal of the advancement of knowledge. Though attacked on all sides, Henry rallied a band of supporters around that banner, and laid the basis for the intellectual advances of future generations of American scientists who, little as

[112] Henry to Bache, June 25, 1852, SI Archives. See also Thomas Coulson, *Joseph Henry: His Life and Work* (Princeton, 1950), 209–10.

[113] Philosophical Society of Washington, *Bulletin*, II (March 1871 to June 1874), reprinted in Smithsonian Miscellaneous Collections, XX (Washington, 1881), xiv.

they understood the history of Henry's fight, clearly comprehended the fundamental necessity for support of basic research untrammeled by practical considerations. In the evolution of institutions, purposes are frequently lost and functions yielded to other institutions. Both of these changes occurred in Smithsonian history. Yet, just as purposes can be lost, so they can be regained. Just as functions can be resigned, so they can be reassumed. Just as the will of Smithson remains unchanged so does the mission of the Institution he founded. The responsibility for remembering the will and executing the mission lies with each succeeding generation, whose faithfulness to the past and responsibility to the present will be interpreted by the historians of each succeeding generation.

A Cabinet of Curiosities

was composed, printed, and bound by
Kingsport Press, Inc., Kingsport, Tennessee.
The types are Century Expanded and
Craw Clarendon Book.
The paper is Mohawk Superfine.
Design is by Edward G. Foss.